GERRY LEKAS

WHERE THE TOUR BUSES DON'T GO

CHICAGO'S Hidden Sites of the Mysterious,
Macabre, Ghostly & Glamorous

GERRY LEKAS

WHERE THE TOUR BUSES DON'T GO

CHICAGO'S Hidden Sites of the Mysterious, Macabre, Ghostly & Glamorous

WITH
PHOTOGRAPHY
BY JOE LEKAS

Black Lyon Publishing, LLC

WHERE THE TOUR BUSES DON'T GO:
CHICAGO'S HIDDEN SITES OF THE MYSTERIOUS,
MACABRE, GHOSTLY AND GLAMOROUS

Black Lyon Travel

*I could never, ever have pulled this off
without the unwavering support of fellow
conspirators Joe Lekas, Liz, Joe, Posey and
Hazel Kozak, Joanne Levine, and of course,
Noreen, the star I have always set my course by.*

"The more outré and grotesque an incident is the more carefully it deserves to be examined."

— Arthur Conan Doyle, "The Hound of the Baskervilles"

TABLE OF CONTENTS

Jack Benny

Abraham Lincoln

Marlon Brando

> *The Farm*
> *His High School*
> *Where he Worked as an Usher*

Bonus: The Rondout Train Robbery

Bonus: Harrison Ford

> *Boyhood Home*

Hillary Rodham Clinton

> *Childhood Home*

John Belushi

> *Boyhood Home*
> *The Belushi Family Plot*

Betty White

Ernest Hemingway

> *Boyhood Home*

Mary Todd Lincoln

> *Where she Lived in Chicago*

Linda Darnell

Harold Ramis

Michael Jordan

Robin Williams

Fred Savage

Mr. T

John Hughes

> Home Alone *House*
> Ferris Bueller's Day Off: *Cameron's House*
> Planes, Trains and Automobiles: *The Neal Page House*
> Dennis the Menace: *Mr. Wilson's House*

Robert Reed

> *Boyhood Home*
> *Grave*

Harry Caray

> *Boyhood Home*

Villa Venice/Rat Pack

7. FURTHER READING & REFERENCES   207

INTRODUCTION

If you're reading this book, I think I can safely make a few assumptions:

• You have a healthy (or, according to your friends and family, decidedly unhealthy) fascination with the darker aspects of the Windy City.

• As a true aficionado of the bizarre and shady underbelly of the city (and surrounding suburbs), you already know a few things about the Chicago Outfit, the St. Valentine's Day Massacre, John Dillinger, H. H. Holmes, John Wayne Gacy, etc., etc., etc.

• You have a robust appreciation of all things paranormal. After all, crime stories and ghost tales seem to go hand-in-hand. In fact, I have yet to meet a true crime buff whose ears don't prick up at the mere mention of paranormal events being connected—even just maybe—to a particular event. Yours probably do, too. Admit it.

• You have almost assuredly visited a few of these sites already, maybe on your own, or by booking passage on one or more of the rather generic and touristy crime or ghost bus tours available.

• Being the enlightened sophisticate you surely are, you have a true appreciation for the cultural icons whose achievements have laid the foundations for our sublime American pop culture. Why, you may have even toured Graceland (or at least considered it). In short, you have a nagging little fascination with celebrities.

Alrighty, then. With this in mind, what I have tried to do

here is to create a self-guided auto tour for you that takes you to the more eclectic Chicago area sites largely unknown (or at least little-known) to most folks.

I have studiously avoided detailed accounts of the more well-known events or locations, except to occasionally touch upon them briefly, in some cases to form context and provide a rationale for suggested visits to alternative (and less touristy), peripheral (but awfully interesting) sites. Why? Several reasons.

First, there are already a ton of really well-done books covering the most well-known crimey and ghosty, sites of Chicago and environs. In addition, there are many, many "ghost tours" and "gangster tours" available to personally escort you there on an air-conditioned bus. Along with a very brief visit to the sites, you are treated to a ton of corny jokes.

Lastly, I wouldn't be the least bit surprised if you have already visited many of the sites already. So, we won't be joining the milling groups looking for faces in the water at the scene of the Eastland Disaster, nor will we be viewing "Death Alley" at the site of the Iroquois Theater Fire of 1903. No Biograph Theater, where John Dillinger bought the farm—but how about a visit to the office where he had his face altered by plastic surgery, or the location where his body was embalmed?

The St. Valentine's Day Massacre? Well, we're not going to actually visit 2122 N. Clark. There's not much to see anyway, just a vacant lot/park next to a retirement home. But you will be provided with a few tasty alternative sites connected to the event that not many know about.

It seems that after the great success of Erik Larson's book, *Devil in the White City*, just about everyone now knows the name of Chicago's notorious H. H. Holmes. But I surely would not recommend visiting the site of his "Murder Castle," on 63rd and Wallace (really dicey neighborhood and no Murder Castle—just a boring post office). Instead, how about a visit to a virtually unknown little site where he constructed an enormous furnace, and quite likely served as a dump site for making the bodies of murder victims disappear?

Along the way, you will learn the details of the horrific

"Big 4" murders that rocked Chicago in the 50s—and changed the city forever.

The dastardly deeds of the Windy City's "Monsters of the Midway" (H. H. Holmes, John Wayne Gacy, Richard Speck, and Williams Heirens) will be covered, as well as a bonus road trip suggestion for visiting the haunts of Wisconsin's Eddie Gein, the real Norman Bates.

In addition, you can view the mansions of many Chicago Outfit mob figures, explore actual haunted area locations, learn the true stories behind notorious crimes, visit the golf course where Bill Murray learned to play, and see Charlton Heston's boyhood home.

That's kind of the gist of this book.

I have not spent an enormous amount of time and ink on elaborate, ponderous life stories of each person and event covered, a lot of which you probably know already. How many times have you waded through a book searching for the juicy bits, only to be subjected to four- or five-page biographies of every person mentioned? Here, I mention really well-known people like John F. Kennedy, Al Capone and Frank Sinatra, and some less known (perhaps) ones like H. H. Holmes and Eddie Gein—and don't feel compelled to relate every minute detail of their lives.

I've always suspected that many authors fatten up the size of their books (the fatter the book, the more gravitas) by filling them with unnecessary stuff (and I may be actually doing a little bit of that now). I am after a more quick-hit, fun read kind of thing here. In this way, I am trying to write a concise little tome that would appeal to me—that lays out the basics and provides a starting point for the reader to delve into more research on the topics that interest them the most—and skips the others.

In short: I have attempted to provide kind of a whirlwind guide to the people, places and events comprising many of the darker (and, in the case of the celebrities/movie stars, glammy) aspects of the Chicago area. I have provided only snapshot descriptions of most people, places and events, so as to cram as many in as possible. They are not painstakingly in-depth—and don't try to be.

What is envisioned: you, dear reader, acquaint yourself a bit with the subjects and sites, choose the ones that tickle your fancy (and would like to visit), fire up the old GPS, and set off on a grand old adventure among some hidden treasures of Chicago history.

One quick note: I toyed with the idea of labeling certain sites "PRDBAJ" (Private Residence: Don't Be A Jerk), but I decided it would be an insult to your intelligence.

Simply please be respectful and unintrusive when nearing a residential or business site.

I can't begin to describe the many agonizing hours I put in attempting to secure permissions for many of the photographs I wanted to include in this section (most notably for the Monsters of the Midway section). Alas, the suits and their lawyers have made the task impossible. In many cases, simply finding out where to go for permissions was a nightmare. In others, paying ridiculous fees would have made the cost of this book somewhere around $3,000 per copy.

So, I have decided to take my own photos, with the assistance of my trusty cohorts, Joe and Noreen, and attempted to capture modern-day looks of sites featured throughout the book.

I highly recommend these three excellent websites:

1. Murderpedia: The Encyclopedia of Murderers https://murderpedia.org. There, you can view a panoply of notorious Chicago killer photos—mug shots, crime scenes, etc. Murderpedia does offer the viewer the opportunity to make a contribution toward site maintenance—so by all means, be the kind and generous person I know you are.

2. My Al Capone Museum: www.myalcaponemuseum. com. Here, you can view a great number of Chicago Mob figures and locations. Mario Gomes has done an excellent job providing photos of significant gangster-related sites.

3. Hogan, Stephen. Chicago Crime Scene Photos, Flickr: www.flickr.com/photos/chicagocrimescenes/albums. Mr. Ho-

gan has done an exhaustive job of locating and photographing extremely hard-to-find crime sites.

1. CREEPY SITES

No, we're not going to talk about Resurrection Mary here. You know, the tired old urban legend about the guy who meets a girl at a dance, starts driving her home, and has her suddenly disappear in front of a cemetery. Why? Well, because in my humble opinion, it's a load of nonsense. There are plenty of tours that will make a big deal out of it if you really want to explore the tale.

Okay, *maybe* I *will* just touch on it a bit.

Resurrection Mary

The ballroom where the fellow supposedly danced with Mary was called the Oh Henry/Willowbrook Ballroom. It burned down in 2016, but I have heard there are plans afoot to restore it. If you really want to visit the spot where it stood, warm up the old GPS:

Oh Henry/Willowbrook Ballroom
8900 Archer Avenue, Willow Springs IL 60480
Now, you see that the ballroom is on Archer Avenue. If you head NE on Archer (the route Mary instructed the fellow to follow toward her home), you will soon reach Resurrection Cemetery.

Resurrection Cemetery
7201 Archer Avenue, Justice IL 60458

The actual identity of Resurrection Mary is a longstanding mystery. The most often-cited candidate is one Mary Bregovy, a girl who was killed in a 1934 car accident while returning from a dance at the O'Henry Ballroom. But there are also other candidates: Ona Norkus, 12, killed in a traffic accident on Archer Avenue in 1927, and Mary Miskowski, who was (supposedly) killed crossing 47th Street on Halloween night, 1930. No one knows for sure who the true Mary was (is).

🔍*Note:* Mary Bregovy is buried at Resurrection Cemetery. Ona Norkus is buried at St. Casimir Cemetery, a few miles SE. Mary Miskowski may not even have been a real person; there's no record of her death or burial.

Chet's Melody Lounge
7400 Archer Avenue, Justice IL 60458
As long as you are there, you should stop in at Chet's Melody Lounge (across the street from the cemetery) for a drink. The locals will be happy (probably?) to regale you with Resurrection Mary tales.

Now if you're ready for some real creepy stuff, here we go!

Bachelor's Grove Cemetery: *The* Haunted Burial Ground

This small cemetery, located in the middle of a forest preserve southwest of Chicago, is not only regarded as one of the most haunted cemeteries in the United States, it's claimed by many to be one of the most haunted in the *world*. World-class creepy!

The area surrounding Bachelor's Grove was settled by immigrants (mostly from New England) around 1833. Burials here began approximately 1834. Reportedly, among the first were German immigrant workers killed while working on the Illinois-Michigan Canal.

The place gradually faded away into obscurity until the

Bachelor's Grove Cemetery: The Mt. Everest of haunted cemeteries.

1950s, when local teenagers began using it as a party spot.

Teenagers, booze and secluded cemeteries are never a good mix. Predictably, vandalism took place and continued well into the 1970s. Tombstones were upheaved, graves were desecrated—there were even reports of satanic rituals being carried out amongst the graves. Soon, the first reports of ghostly phenomena began being reported. It was thought that, quite reasonably, the utter desecration of the site triggered the disturbances.

Bachelor's Grove soon became a common watchword among Chicagoans (especially teenagers) as *the* spot for spooky goings-on, and of course, began drawing even more of the curious. Gradually, the police and forest preserve agents began a more energetic patrolling of the area, and order was restored (kind of).

However, the ghostly phenomena continue to this day. A few of the reported sightings highlights:

• A ghostly farmhouse that appears along the winding trail through the woods leading to the cemetery. Witnesses have claimed it appears in distinct detail, down to lights in the windows and even a front porch swing. The best part? The farmhouse fades and finally disappears as you draw closer.

• Ghostly orbs of light that both bounce along the trail and appear within the cemetery itself.

• Just to the north of the cemetery (beyond the fence) is a small lagoon. There have been numerous sightings of the ghostly figure of a farmer plowing the area next to the lagoon behind an equally ghostly-looking horse. Some witnesses have claimed that upon being seen, the ghost horse will suddenly spook and plunge into the water, dragging farmer and plow.

• A sobbing Woman in White, aka The Madonna, often carrying an infant, has been reported wandering amongst the graves.

• A very odd occurrence was first reported by two ghost researchers attempting to spend the night in the cemetery. They claimed that in the early morning hours, a fierce storm broke out suddenly with trees bending under the wind and rain pelting down.

Okay, not so weird, right? Just a storm. But how about this: As they looked beyond the surrounding fence, they saw that the storm was confined to just the grounds of the cemetery itself!

• Faces have often been reported appearing—and then disappearing—upon a particular gravestone/monument (Fulton). The Fulton monument is the tall one toward the far-left side of the cemetery.

❀ *Personal Note:* I've always had really rotten luck with ghost stuff. I don't know, maybe I'm just not receptive enough, wired right, or tuned in properly. But, I will tell you that even I could sense *something* inside the gates of Bachelor's Grove. There's just something about the atmosphere. For one thing, the very air within that relatively small area seems … different. Heavy. While the trail leading to the cemetery is brimming with life—insects humming, squirrels and chipmunks dashing around, and tree branches swaying in the breeze—that all seems to stop once you enter the gates. It's unmistakable. I have never seen any small wildlife within that cemetery.

See what you think.

🚐 *How to Get There:* Bachelor's Grove Cemetery (actual address): 5900 W. Midlothian Turnpike/143rd Street, Midlothian, IL 60445. (But you will park in the Rubio Woods lot on the north side of 143rd Street.)

The best way to get there is to set your GPS for the Rubio Woods Forest Preserve.

Rubio Woods Forest Preserve. W. Midlothian Turnpike/W. 143rd Street (west of S. Ridgeland Avenue) Cook County, IL 60445 (near Midlothian).

Try to get a spot as soon as you pull in the lot. Once you've parked, find the path running right along Midlothian/143Road Head west along the path for about 100 yards or so, keeping your eyes out for a metal chain crossing an opening into the woods on the south side of the street. Once you locate it, carefully cross the street. Traffic can be tricky here, so be cautious.

You will now find a path beyond the metal chain leading into the woods. Follow it. You will need to travel about one-quarter of a mile to reach the cemetery. Along the way, notice how the overhanging trees make walking the trail seem like traveling through a murky tunnel. Also, take note of the wild-life sounds and activity going on in the woods all around you, which will change remarkably once you enter the cemetery.

Along this path, witnesses have claimed to see the vanishing farmhouse, just off to the right or left in the woods. Oh, if you see it? Don't attempt to approach it. Local legends claim that if you actually manage to enter it, you will never be seen again. You know—a Hotel California/Roach Motel kind of thing. "You can check in, but you can't check out."

Also, keep an eye out for the bouncing orbs of light, often blue and red, seen by observers. They are said to appear along the trail at all hours.

You will soon see a slight bend in the trail toward the

right. As you follow it, the gates and fence of Bachelor's Grove loom in the mist (only if it's misty out, of course).

Step through those gates. You're on your own now. Good luck.

Read-Dunning Memorial Park/ Dunning Cemetery
**Intersection of W. Belleplaine Avenue & N. Neenah Avenue
Chicago IL 60634**

Read Dunning Memorial Park. Thousands of Chicago's poor, insane, and orphaned rest here.

This small park/cemetery is surely one of the saddest and most forlorn you will ever visit. In the first place, there's its history. It was the burial ground for an insane asylum, poorhouse, and tuberculosis hospital. Secondly, its odd location: secluded yet curiously right in the midst of a ring of condominiums and single-family homes, right off Narragansett Avenue and Irving Park Road on the city's Northwest side. Most Chicagoans are not even aware of its existence.

This was a small portion of the site known as Dunning to

the people in my northwest side neighborhood—the infamous insane asylum around which countless dark rumors were spoken of as gospel. Any nut-brained or rebellious kid behavior was met with the parental admonishment: "You are one small step away from us shipping you off to Dunning."

Around the mid-1850s, this area was set aside by Chicago city fathers as a work farm/poorhouse, called the County Farm, for the destitute. An infirmary and insane asylum were added in 1870. A cemetery was soon needed, not only for those who died here, but for the many dead being shipped here for reinternment from Chicago's own City Cemetery, now Lincoln Park.

As the city grew and spread out, there were concerns that a cemetery close to the main population hub would be a threat to drinking water. A special train line was run out to the Dunning area to transport not only displaced bodies, but also many destitute and mentally-troubled folks that Chicago simply wanted out of the way. Northwest-siders, well known for their refined sensitivities, dubbed this "the crazy train."

Living conditions here were routinely horrible: poor or little care, overcrowding, rough treatment, and weevil-infested food. There were instances of troublesome patients/inmates being placed under constant sedation with choral hydrate, or even beaten to death by the staff. On-the-take attendants even arranged for some recently-dead to be purchased by so-called "resurrectionists," medical school representatives seeking bodies for anatomical training purposes. A *Chicago Tribune* reporter wrote that the inmates of the poorhouse were "crowded and herded together like sheep in the shambles, and hogs in the slaughtering-pens."[1] In perhaps the most accurate indictment of the place, a judge in 1894 referred to it as "a tomb for the living."

Over time, circumstances changed, and so did the land and buildings. The County sold the property to the State in 1912, and burial records stopped being kept. The old structures were soon replaced by the new facilities of the Chicago State Hospital, and later the Chicago-Read Hospital.

This part is really weird: as time went by, everyone

seemed to completely forget about the entire giant cemetery. It wasn't until 1989, when developers purchased large portions of the land for the construction of new housing and began digging foundations, that there was a collective official "uh oh."

Bodies were turning up with almost every swipe of the bulldozers.

Uh oh, indeed. "Nowhere else in the country has a cemetery with hundreds or thousands of graves been so nearly forgotten that a developer had to rediscover it by accident,"[2] wrote a Chicago Reader reporter in September of 1989.

Nevertheless, the developers persisted, although with a more scaled-back approach. Fewer homes were constructed than originally planned for.

The park itself is not all that much—mostly open land with a few stone plaques in the ground commemorating the many dead buried here over the years. And there were lots of them. Lots. Considerably more than the somewhat conservative estimate of 38,000.

Once you enter the park, simply stand and take in the view for 360 degrees. Under the land you are now surrounded by (including those single-family houses to the south and condos to the east), lie the unmarked graves containing the remains of countless unknown and forgotten souls: the poor, the insane, orphaned and abandoned children, unknown victims of the Chicago Fire of 1871, and a few executed criminals to boot.

The bodies of those hanged in the city were often sent here. When developers purchased the land in 1989 and began laying the foundations for those homes you see all around, they began uncovering body after body. After body. After body. And there is absolutely no doubt they missed plenty. The area to the west, beyond the medical facility buildings and reaching all the way to Oak Park Boulevard, was all part of the Dunning complex, and undoubtedly also used for burials. (38,000 bodies is a lot of bodies).

There is a very real aura of melancholy about the park. Various stones will mention the different groups of dead all spending eternity here, and the thought of the many poor, orphaned and abandoned kids buried here is especially heart-breaking.

There have been reports of ghostly phenomena here from time to time (given the circumstances, that should come as no surprise), but seem pretty uniformly non-threatening. Visitors often claim to have heard disembodied voices in the distance.

M. Julia Buccola Petta: The Incorruptible Italian Bride
Mount Carmel Cemetery, 1400 S. Wolf Road
Hillside IL 60162

This one is not really scary—but it's definitely odd. Julia Buccola Petta, married only the year before in Chicago, died in childbirth (along with her baby) on March 17, 1921—a not-so-unusual but still tragic occurrence in those times. She was buried here at Mt. Carmel, holding her son, and dressed in the same gown she had been married in. A sad story, to be sure, and it should have ended there, but it did not.

Shortly after Julia's death, her mother, Filomena, began being tormented by the same nightmare night after night. In the terrifying dream, Julia claimed she was not really dead and pleaded for her help. Filomena unsuccessfully attempted to have her daughter's body exhumed for six long years, as the nightmares continued. At last, a sympathetic judge granted her request, and the grave was opened.

When the rotting casket lid was lifted, it revealed an astonishing sight: the body of Julia Buccola Petta was virtually free of all signs of decomposition, while the body of the infant in her arms had decayed badly. It was said that her skin was as soft and unmarked as it had been when she was alive. A photograph of her was taken. For all the world, the photo appears to show a woman merely asleep, not dead and buried for six long years. This photograph, above the words "Presa Dopo 6 Anni Morta" (Taken 6 Years After Death) would be affixed to her grave monument upon her reburial.

The family took the incorruptibility of Julia's body to be a miracle from God; many others now considered her an actual saint. Money poured in for a new, impressive stone monument, which still stands at the grave today. Filomena apparently did not approve of her former son-in-law; the grave is marked as that of "Julia Buccola."

There are a few ghost sightings connected to this tale involving Julia. In the most poignant one, a young child, accidentally left behind at the cemetery by his family, explained when found that he had held the hand of a mysterious dark haired lady—who faded away when his frantic parents returned.

The St. Rita's Church Incident: One Very Unusual Day
6243 S. Fairfield Avenue, Chicago IL 60629

Admittedly, this one has more than a modicum of ghostly urban legend to it. In fact, the date of the supposed incident can't even be firmly established. Best guess: 1961. But it is claimed by quite a few older Southside neighborhood residents that on one particular All Soul's Day (November 2) sometime in the early 1960s, a very terrifying incident occurred. And the particulars of this tale are so compellingly outre that even if the events never happened—dammit—they should have.

Here's the story: On that fateful All Soul's Day, about a dozen congregants were praying for the souls of the dearly departed in the church. Suddenly, from the loft above the church entrance, the organ began playing. The parishioners looked up to see six semi-transparent cloaked figures gathered around the organ, three shrouded in white, three in black.

The congregation panicked and stampeded for the doors, but they wouldn't open. Terrified, they looked back in horror as the six figures gently floated down from the loft to the main floor. As they drifted over the pews toward the altar, they were heard to say, "Pray for us."

At that moment, the doors were flung open by a strong

wind and the shocked parishioners spilled outside.

And that was the end of it. No further ghostly incidents were ever reported at St. Rita's. Make of the story what you will, but there are still neighborhood residents who swear the tale is true.

Note: One of the nice things about church sites is they don't change much over the years. St. Rita's still looks about the same as it did in 1962.

St. James at Sag Bridge Cemetery
10600 Archer Avenue, Lemont IL 60439

If you dialed up central casting and ordered a haunted cemetery set, St. James at the Sag is what you would get— and be quite pleased with. Simply put, this boneyard is what a haunted cemetery should look like. Far more atmospheric (at first glance) than my personal favorite, Bachelor's Grove. The St. James features lots and lots of very old tombstones sur-

St. James at Sage Bridge certainly looks the part of a haunted grave-yard.

rounding a church perched on a hill.

St. James sits upon a bluff overlooking the juncture of the (now called) Calumet Sag Channel and the Chicago Sanitary and Ship Canal. When French explorers had visited this exact spot in 1673, they learned that the native Indians had already been using the bluff as sacred burial grounds for some time. It is believed that famed French cleric/explorer Father Jacques Marquette himself had celebrated a mass upon the bluff.

In 1836, work had started on the construction of a waterway that was to link the Great Lakes with the Mississippi River, which was to be called the Illinois-Michigan Canal. The first church was constructed here at about the same time by Irish Catholic workers (and local farmers) to minister to the needs of the growing number of men working on the project. Many of the graves you will find here contain their earthly remains.

Ghost stories have been associated with St. James since at least as far back as 1897. The Chicago Tribune reported then that two young Chicago musicians had performed a concert at the church one evening, and decided to spend the night. They were said to have been awakened in the dead of night by the sound of hoofs pounding up the driveway outside. Looking out a window, they observed two figures, a man and a girl in white, within a ghostly carriage.

The two musicians watched the carriage gallop away into nothingness. Locals were quick to suggest that what the two men had seen were the ghosts of a St. James' priest's assistant and a housemaid, who had fallen in love long ago and arranged to elope. Tragically, the carriage they had left in had overturned close to the church, killing them both (they were said to have been buried in unmarked graves in the churchyard). On moonlit nights, the two lovers are said to be often seen attempting to complete their doomed elopement.

St. James also has reports of monk-like figures roaming the churchyard, threatening visitors. In one particularly compelling account the belligerent monk in question was actually named. According to locals, the ghost of Rev. George Aschenbrenner still haunts the grounds, scaring off interlopers.

Note: As late as 1977, reports of ghostly, black-robed monks were still being filed—even by the police!

Old Town Tatu
3313 W. Irving Park Road, Chicago IL 60618

As I mentioned in the Introduction, I'm not going to recommend visiting lame ghost sites, those supposedly steeped in paranormal activities—but really not. We shall leave those for the tour buses. You may have noticed that almost all ghost tours in Chicago seem to find their terrifically haunted sites within a very narrow radius surrounding downtown hotels. It's probably only a sheer coincidence that this is exactly where the preponderance of visitors to our lovely Windy City happen to stay.

But enough of that. How about a visit to a former funeral parlor in the Old Irving Park area that actually does seem to be rife with haunted goings-on?

Old Town Tatu was once the Klemundt Funeral Parlor. There seems to be some debate over how old the structure really is, and how long it housed the business. In 2003, the building was converted to a tattoo parlor, and it was then that strange phenomena occurrences kicked into high gear.

The new owner, Richie "Tapeworm" Herrera, and his staff reported objects being thrown about, strange noises, erratically-functioning appliances and even incidents of employees being pushed by unseen hands. It was thought that the conversion of this former house of death into a tattoo parlor did not sit well with spirits still residing here.

A paranormal investigation team identified at least three ghostly entities: "Walter," who may have been the original owner, a strange and somewhat violent man clad in a rather old-fashioned suit, and a little girl.

Ritchie Herrera grew annoyed with the more physical incidences of his unseen residents. After being pushed on a staircase by unseen hands, he swore that if he happened to ever die in the shop, he would return from the afterlife to "kick [his tormenter's] ass." Sadly, in 2006, Herrera did indeed die in the shop—a mere three weeks after making his promise.

Herrera seems to have made good on his vow. Remaining employees report that his presence is constantly felt in the shop. And it didn't take long. Shortly after his death, a group of his friends were at the shop when the phone rang. The number on caller ID was that of Ritchie Herrera despite the fact that the number had been disconnected after his passing.

In addition, Tapeworm's old tattoo station, if manned by a new employee, will often be beset by unidentifiable equipment malfunctions. On the other hand, if the operator is someone he knew and liked in life, the equipment functions smoothly.

✐ Notes:

1. Old Town Tatu is well worth a visit. Employees there are friendly and seem quite open to sharing their stories.

2. The basement, where bodies were once stored (as well as being embalmed) is said to be especially spooky and subject to poltergeist activity.

Our Lady of Angels
3820 W. Iowa Street, Chicago IL 60651

On December 1, 1958, one of the greatest tragedies in Chicago history occurred, permanently scarring this west side neighborhood with a sorrow from which it has never fully recovered. On that date, a horrific fire swept with astonishing speed through the two-story Catholic elementary school that once stood on this site, claiming the lives of 92 pupils and three nuns.

At approximately 2:40 PM, children were nearing the end of their school day 20 minutes away. Two students returning from an errand reported smelling smoke in the halls. Two classes immediately evacuated the building, but other classrooms were not even aware of the situation. By the time they were, smoke and heat, particularly on the second floor, had made conditions for evacuation virtually impossible. Children panicked, stumbling through the halls; some jumped out windows to the frozen ground 25 feet below.

Seeing the chaos, at least one nun instructed her students to remain at their desks and pray for rescue. The students on the first floor were far luckier, spilling out the doors into the street.

By the time fire trucks began arriving at the scene, the building had become a raging inferno. Firefighters would never forget the faces of screaming children at the second floor windows. Some were urged to jump into waiting arms below, but others were too afraid to try.

In heroic desperation, firemen threw ladders up against the walls and scrambled up to yank as many children out through the windows as they could.

Despite their best efforts, the mission of the first responders would soon change from rescue to recovery. Many children's bodies would be found still at their desks inside charred classrooms.

There were many reasons for this tragedy. In 1958, there were no school smoke detectors or sprinkler systems. In addition, fire escapes were woefully inadequate, and the stairway landing doors were wide open instead of closed, allowing the fire to spread rapidly. It was determined later that the blaze had begun near a basement staircase. Exacerbating things, the building, constructed in 1910, had a roof that had been tarred over many times; it was so thick that the fire could not burn through it, releasing some of the deadly smoke and heat.

But by 1958 standards, the school building was safe. In a truly tragic bit of irony, Our Lady of Angels School had passed a fire inspection just two months previously.

The Archdiocese of Chicago, responsible for city Catholic schools, was never held legally accountable for the disaster. The tragedy was simply declared to be "God's Will."

Reports of ghostly phenomena began even as the fire raged at this site. A frantic mother, rushing to the scene, was relieved to see her smiling son running toward her from the school. Before she could reach him, they were separated by the crowd. Only later did she learn that the boy had perished in his second-floor classroom. A boy searching for his sister near the school saw her walking happily toward home. She too, would later prove to be a victim of the fire. Other parents of victims would claim that their children would visit them as they slept. Several victims' siblings reported that they were often comforted by the spirits of dead brothers and sisters.

Visitors to this area occasionally report the sounds of screams and moans, as well as the faint odor of smoke.

🔑 *Notes:*

1.   A new Our Lady of Angels school (with modern safety devices) was eventually built on the site, but it closed in 1999. The building was then used as a charter school, which would fall victim to the Illinois budget in 2016.

2.   A memorial to the victims of the Our Lady of Angels victims, as well as the graves of 25 victims, can be found at Queen of Heaven Cemetery in Hillside. Address: Queen of Heaven Cemetery Memorial (Section 18), 1400 S. Wolf Road, Hillside, IL 60162.

The odor of smoke is also sometimes noticed near the memorial.

The Victorian House
806 W. Belmont Avenue, Chicago IL 60657

Built in 1879, this stately Victorian-style edifice stands like a jewel amidst the more modern structures on Belmont. Originally a residence for a well-to-do Chicago family of a bygone time, it eventually became a speakeasy during the 1920s. Later, it became an antique store, and things began to get way more interesting.

By the 1970s, owner Al Morlock was in charge, and he hired two of my friends to help out. Darryl and Bobby spent a lot of time here, primarily lugging heavy Victorian chests and tables up and down the stairs. I visited them here on many occasions and through Morlock, learned something of the history of the building.

Besides the speakeasy stuff, there were lots of ghostly go-ings-on there that kept everyone on edge. Unexplained noises and voices were heard constantly, mostly emanating from the upstairs floor. Two old portraits, ostensibly of a man and his wife, hung near a staircase and made both employees and customers extremely uneasy—although no one could explain exactly why. These portraits were eventually sold to a restaurant interior designer, who placed them in another allegedly haunted location, That Steak Joynt (now closed).

Morlock, troubled by the atmosphere at his business, de-cided to research the history of the building. He learned that a woman had been murdered here in the 1880s and four people had later perished in an attic fire. Morlock became convinced these entities had chosen to remain at The Victorian House.

🔑*Note:* Although there was a genuinely eerie quality to the rooms of The Victorian House, I never noticed any specific phenomena (although as I have previously mentioned, I am not particularly receptive). Al Morlock has since left this mortal coil, but Darryl and Bobby can still relate countless encounters with spirits here.

An apartment rental firm now occupies the space.

═══ The Crash of Flight 191 ═══
320 W. Touhy Avenue, Des Plaines IL 60018

On May 25, 1979, American Airlines flight 191, bound for Los Angeles, took off from nearby O'Hare Airport at 3 PM. As the DC10 sped down runway 32R, the left-wing engine suddenly tore loose and crashed to the ground. The crew were possibly unaware of this at first, as the plane lifted off and struggled to gain altitude. But one of the pilots quickly became aware; the last word heard on the flight recorder was "Damn!"[3]

As the plane reached an altitude of about 300 feet, it suddenly pitched left, then turned over and plummeted to the ground.

Flight 191, after only 31 seconds in the air, crashed into a field here, a few hundred yards north of the Touhy Avenue Mobile Homes Park, killing all 271 passengers and crew, plus two men on the ground.

A huge explosion rocked the area, and a ball of fiery smoke erupted at the crash site, visible for miles. It was obvious to first-responders arriving at the site that there could be no survivors. Even the most veteran of police officers would later describe the scene as the most horrible thing they had ever seen. When searching for victims, a first responder had to ask a pathologist for help in even identifying smoldering objects as body parts. They simply looked like large, life-sized clumps of black coal. What remains could be found were placed in plastic bags and transported back to O'Hare, which was now functioning as a temporary morgue.

Almost immediately after the crash site investigation and after cleanup efforts had been completed, the first reports of unnatural activities from the area began coming in. Motorists traveling along both Touhy and Elmhurst Road were phoning in to police to state that they had observed flickering orbs of light hovering in the crash area. In addition, dogs housed at a nearby police canine training facility, as well as the pets of the mobile home community residents, were barking endlessly at the field where the plane had gone down. Even more disturbing were the reports from the homeowners themselves. Many were reporting loud knocks at their doors in the middle of the night. When they answered—there was no one there. They also were claiming that moans and wailing were sometimes heard outside.

Undoubtedly the most eerie: a man walking his dog near the area one chilly night reported that he had been confronted by an agitated young man asking where the nearest phone booth could be found. He claimed he needed to make an emergency call. The dog-walker was startled to notice the young man's clothes appeared to be steaming—and reeked strongly of gas. Before directions to the nearest phone could be explained, the young man faded away into nothingness.

The crash site lies north of the police K9 training facility on Touhy, east of the mobile home park. A memorial wall honoring the dead: Lake Park, 1201 E. Touhy, Des Plaines, 60018.

Note: On the afternoon of May 25, 1979, I was traveling west on Golf Road, just a bit north of O'Hare on my way to a movie theater near Woodfield Shopping Center (to see *Alien*). It must have been shortly after the crash, because I certainly heard no explosion. I did, however, see a cloud of smoke to the south. It wasn't till I returned home later that I learned of the tragedy.

Robinson Woods
4830-4870 N. East River Road, Chicago IL 60706

Alexander Robinson (approximately 1789-1872) was the Americanized name of Che-che-pin-quay, an important Indian leader in northern Illinois. His mother was a member of the Ottawa tribe. His father was a Scotch trader.

Robinson was of inestimable value to the American newcomers from the East, now settling in the Chicagoland environs. He served as interpreter, liaison and mediator between the settlers and members of the Potowatomie, Chippewa, Odawa and other tribes living in the area. Undoubtedly, his greatest service occurred in 1812, when he rescued and protected survivors of the Fort Dearborn Massacre, transporting them to areas of safety. He would go to work as a fur trader and treaty negotiator, often proving of assistance to the U.S. Army.

In appreciation of his services, Robinson was granted a large, 1,280-acre tract of land along the Des Plaines River. He spent his last years here, often regaling visitors with a favorite story about once meeting Abraham Lincoln. Descendants of Robinson lived on the property until May 1955, when a fire destroyed their home. Several members of the family, including Alexander Robinson himself, were buried here.

Over the years, there have been many stories about strange phenomena in this area. People have reported a wide

The guardians of Robinson Woods.

variety of experiences, including strange sights, sounds, and smells. And always: a feeling of being watched.

The area around the memorial stone commemorating Robinson and his clan seem to serve as a focal point for the activities. Two paths lead off into the woods from here. The one to the left follows the route the Robinsons would take to the Des Plaines River to get water. It is along this path that bobbing orbs of light are often seen. Some late-night visitors have reported the odor of campfires in the air and even the sound of drums in the distance.

Another more uncommon occurrence involves the behavior of deer in the area. Unlike most deer, the ones populating this forest area seem unafraid of humans, at times following (or shadowing) visitors for fairly long distances.

All those legends about restless Indian burial grounds seem to really do apply at this site.

🔍 *Note:* I paid a visit here in October 2019. A deer, sporting pretty impressive antlers, appeared at the memorial stone as soon as I started heading back to my car. He stood motionless, watching me intently until I pulled away.

Eerie.

I just returned from a follow-up visit here (February, 2020). This time, nine or ten deer roamed the memorial stone area. At my approach, all stood stock-still, watching.

Eerie 2.0.

✺ *Bonus:* My own little brush with ghosts in Richmond, 10321 N. Main Street, Richmond IL 60071 (now Main Street Coffee).

Okay, this one is all me. You aren't going to find any haunted info on this building, just business reviews about lattes and cappuccinos. You're just going to have to trust me here. Or not, of course.

As I mentioned earlier, I am just not very susceptible to paranormal vibes. No matter how many notoriously ghostly hot spots I visit, my psychic radar almost invariably remains irritatingly flat. Over the years I've slept in supposedly-haunted castles in Europe, spent evenings exploring London's Jack the Ripper locations, poked around the creepy underground vaults beneath Edinburgh, booked rooms at insane-asylums-turned-hotels, and traipsed through countless deserted graveyards. As much as I've tried to keep my paranormal channels open, virtually nothing.

Except in this building.

Some years ago, my wife and I passed through Richmond, located very near the Illinois/Wisconsin border, on a pleasure drive. At that time, Richmond's Main Street was home to a few interesting-looking antique shops. This two-story brick building was one of them.

I'm not sure how old it is, but it's old. Embedded in the wooden floor was an enormous and ancient iron grate, which apparently was used for the circulation of air long ago. A flight of stairs led up to the second floor, which, the proprietor informed us, had once served as a town dance hall. More antiques could be viewed there. At the top of the landing, a wooden ticket booth stood near the doorways to two large rooms. My wife chose one and I chose the other.

Within a few minutes, a feeling of oppression and sadness tugged at me. In addition, I experienced a very distinct feeling of being watched. I just didn't want to be in that room. Hurrying from it, I met my wife leaving briskly from the other room.

We compared notes, and found that we had both experienced exactly the same feelings.

Now, I know it's not much, but when even such a hardheaded, psychically-challenged insensitive (and my wife is pretty much the same) gets the willies (for the first time ever)—well, maybe that's something!

Note: The building has housed different businesses since its antique store days. As of 2019, it's a coffeehouse.

The Lobstein House
905 Elgin Avenue, Forest Park IL 60130

John George Lobstein, a Chicago lumber mill giant, built this Victorian painted-lady home in the 1890s. His wife, Adaline (or Addy) died in the house, supposedly from childbirth complications. The child, Eddie, was said to have gone insane and to have hung himself at age 12 in the attic. Addy and Eddie are thought to be the entities now haunting the building.

Whatever the circumstances, the 11-room, 4,100 square-foot mansion has been regarded as a genuinely haunted house for many, many years. Shadows are often seen flitting about the attic, as well as unexplained noises. Cold spots appear at different places in the home, and the sound of a child's footsteps can sometimes be heard coming from the upstairs bedrooms. Neighbors have reported seeing a ghostly figure peering down from an upstairs window. A psychic brought in by a previous owner, upon touching a fireplace mantel, picked up the name "Addy," as well as the words "lumber mill."

For some unknown reason, every November 6 seems to trigger a host of paranormal activity. On that date, a number of the curious arrive at the area in hopes of observing something otherworldly.

Note: A family lived here continuously for 27 years, so it must be assumed that the spirits residing within are of the harmless variety.

Hotel Baker
100 W. Main Street, St. Charles IL 60174

The Hotel Baker is an absolute gem of a hotel, situated on the banks of the Fox River. It was the dream project of a man named Edward J. Baker, who purchased land once occupied in 1837 by a mill, and later, garbage dump. Baker, dubbed "The Colonel," loved St. Charles and wanted to create an opulent, yet relatively inexpensive showplace to bring visitors to the town.

Baker inherited a vast sum of money (38 million dollars) upon the death of a sister, Dellora, in 1918. Dellora was the widow of a fascinating character named John "Bet a Million" Gates, who was the founder of the Texaco Oil Company. His nickname came from his penchant for outrageous gambling, at which he was extremely successful. He once made a large bet that one raindrop would drip down a window faster than another. Upon the death of Gates in 1911, his estate passed to his wife and son. When son Charlie died in 1913 and wife Delora in 1918, the Gates fortune was inherited by Colonel Baker.

In 1926, Baker began the construction of his dream hotel, and on June 2, 1928, it opened for business. The Colonel spared no expense: the Hotel Baker featured its own radio station, miniature golf course, gardens, and "The Rainbow Room"—a restaurant/ballroom with an electrically controlled dance floor sporting ever-changing colored lights. Top national bands led by Louis Armstrong, Lawrence Welk, Tommy Dorsey and Guy Lombardo played the room. Outside, colorful spotlights illuminated the adjacent Fox River.

Baker operated the Hotel Baker joyfully, despite never turning a profit. Upon his death in 1959, the property began a period of decline. Without Baker's guiding hand, the hotel could not maintain its former glory.

In 1970, his daughter donated the building to a Lutheran social services group, who converted it to an assisted-living facility. Upkeep could not be maintained; artwork and furniture was sold off to stave off closure.

The building would eventually be sold twice, first to two St. Charles businessmen who renovated it at great expense and reopened it. After failing to make a profitable go of it, the property went into foreclosure and was purchased by a young and energetic couple who run it now.

Ghostly Phenomena: The primary haunting presence is thought to be the spirit of a hotel chambermaid who was jilted by her lover either at the altar or following a losing poker game.

She allegedly committed suicide by throwing herself into the Fox River just east of the hotel. Moans can sometimes be heard from a sixth-floor storage area. In addition, some guests have reported bedding being tugged by an unseen force.

There are also those who claim that old Colonel Edward Baker himself is still keeping an eye on things at Hotel Baker. After his wife's death, The Colonel moved into the hotel, occupying rooms on the fifth floor. A gauzy apparition, said to closely resemble him, has occasionally been seen upon a staircase.

The Red Geranium
19 W. Benton Avenue, Naperville IL 60540

Sadly, the spot once occupied by a small house known as The Red Geranium is now just a tiny vacant lot. For many years, a small, brightly-colored stucco house stood here. Back in the 1990s, it housed an interior decoration/landscape design business called The Red Geranium. But the building was originally a residence—with a tragic legacy.

On October 15, 1984, a young resident of the home, Lawrence V. Phillips, was found dead in the basement. His death was ruled a suicide by carbon monoxide and methane poisoning.

The later owner of the building converted it to a business, first called Homespun Interiors and then The Red Geranium. A feng shui specialist was engaged to assist with the conversion. While touring the site, she was stopped in her tracks when approaching the basement, declaring she could not enter the area.

A paranormal investigator was brought in. His infrared-light video footage captured a dark shadow with a human shape climbing the stairs leading up from the basement before dissolving into an orb of light and passing into the kitchen.

The business moved out of the building in 2004, relocating to a new location. The house remained empty for 13 long years, boarded up and decaying, but its reputation as a genuine haunted site continued to grow. Neighbors and passers-by continuously reported seeing a shadow peering out of the windows, especially as night fell. The shadow has most often been described as having the form of a slender man.

Teenagers began breaking into the house in search of the ghost. City fathers eventually decided that enough was enough, and the building fell to the wreckers' ball. But just because it's no longer there might not ensure that the resident ghost has moved on.

Note: My son and I visited the site several years ago when the house was still there. As we stood on the sidewalk facing it on a dark fall night, the doorknob of the front door suddenly began to violently rattle. The house was boarded up and dark. I seriously doubt anyone (at least living) waited patiently inside just to prank us. I have to admit we were both creeped out.

As long as you are in Naperville, two more sites:

The Naperville Train Disaster
Loomis St. & 4th Avenue, Naperville IL 60540

On April 26, 1946, a horrific train crash here claimed the lives of 45 people and injured 125 more. Two southwest-bound trains left Chicago within minutes of each other along the same track.

Around 1 PM, the lead train, experiencing mechanical difficulties, stopped here. For unknown reasons, the following train missed frantic warning attempts and plowed into it. Many passengers occupying the rear section of the lead train were killed outright and many more in the forward cars were severely injured. Witnesses would later recount that the screams and moans from the victims were unearthly.

Workers from a nearby furniture factory raced to the scene and began pulling mangled bodies from the wreck, even before police and fire units could arrive. It's said that the dead and injured were placed upon the lawns up and down Loomis Street.

Kroehler Furniture Factory: Temporary Morgue/Hospital
200 E. 5th Avenue, Naperville IL 60540
(now 5th Avenue Station)
The 800 employees of this factory (now converted to an apartment/retail complex) heroically came to the aid of the crash victims. As rescue and medical personnel arrived, the building was hastily transformed into an emergency hospital—and soon, morgue.

Note: Whenever people (especially a large group) lose their lives completely unexpectedly—and violently—it's not unreasonable that the surroundings manage to retain a residue of the shock and suffering experienced. It's said that a walk down Loomis Avenue, where the bodies of dead, dying, and badly injured victims were strewn upon the lawns, can be an eerie experience.

Naperville Grave Robbing
105 S. Ellsworth Avenue, Naperville IL 60540

Admittedly, this one has a certain urban legend vibe to it. Over the years, so many fantastic embellishments have attached themselves to the story of Charles Hillegas that it's become difficult to separate truth from legend. In effect, the embellishments have served to transform a genuinely bizarre tale into something bordering on the outlandish. Yet, compelling evidence exists to support at the least the bones of the story.

The facts: A young man from a wealthy Naperville family relocated to Seattle with a woman named Jesse (it's unclear if they were legally married) in the early years of the 20th Century. She died in 1912, and a distraught Charles transported her back home for burial at the Naperville Cemetery.

Naperville Cemetery
705 S. Washington St., Naperville IL 60540
Supposedly, shortly after the internment, Charles Hillegas became convinced Jesse was not really dead. According to contemporary newspaper accounts, he became hysterical at the cemetery, loudly shouting that she was alive even as her casket was being lowered into the ground.

Friends, fearing for his sanity, brought him back to his parents' home and kept a close watch over him. At some point, he managed to arm himself and slip away. Hillegas traveled back to the cemetery, where he dug up Jesse's remains. He transported the body to the family home here on Ellsworth Avenue, placed it in the adjacent barn, and guarded it. His friends soon became aware and tried to reason with him, but to no avail.

The sheriff and his staff were soon called upon to resolve the situation, and arrived on the scene. Jesse's body was returned to the cemetery for reburial. Charles Hillegas was sent off to a mental institution. He would eventually be buried beside Jesse in the Naperville Cemetery family plot.

As if this tale was not macabre enough, certain wild flourishes added to it by locals took it to fantastic new heights. It was soon being said that Charles Hillegas dabbled in chemistry and had become convinced he had created a potion that could actually return the dead to life. It was whispered he had brought Jesse corpse to the barn in order to resuscitate it with the potion. It was also later claimed that he had lived in the barn with the corpse for weeks.

As time passed, still another version of the story developed that had Jesse dying years earlier than she actually did. In this version, Hillegas only perfected his life-restoring potion long after her death; he exhumed her rotting corpse 18 long years after her burial. Apparently, this version of the story simply sprang from later confusion regarding the dates on Hillegas family tombstones, and cannot be taken seriously.

The outlandish embroideries actually only serve to detract from the actual facts of the event, which are certainly bizarre enough on their own.

Paranormal phenomena: Visitors to Naperville Cemetery, where Charles & Jesse rest, often report observing dancing orbs of light glowing near the gravesites. They appear randomly at all hours, often blinking on and off before fading away. In addition, the filmy apparition of an old woman is sometimes seen soon after winter storms walking barefoot through the snow before abruptly vanishing.

The Hillegas house on Ellsworth Avenue (the barn is long gone) certainly looks a bit spooky, but not much in the way of supernatural activity has been reported. Even so, it's pretty cool to take a late-evening stroll past it and recall the events that took place here over one hundred years ago.

The Schweppe Mansion
405 N. Mayflower Road, Lake Forest, IL 60045

The North Shore area is littered with mansions, but this one is a *mansion*. Constructed in 1917 for a staggering cost, this 27-room palace was a wedding gift from Marshall Field chairman John G. Shedd to his daughter, Laura, and new husband,

Charles Schweppe.

The opulent home, one might think, should have been the setting for happily-ever-after stuff, but it didn't work out that way.

For a while, all was fine. The Schweppes often threw lavish parties, sometimes attended by royalty. At one such gala, the Swedish crown prince and princess danced the night away on the mansion's eastern terrace. Edward, Duke of Windsor (the recently-abdicated King of England,) and the woman he spurned the crown for, Wallis Simpson, were overnight guests here.

But things may not have been all they seemed at the Schweppe Mansion. In 1937, Laura died. Instead of her large estate (valued at over $10 million) passing directly to her husband, the bulk of the money went to her children. Charles received a paltry $200,000.

Four years after Laura's death, a troubled Charles committed suicide in an upstairs bedroom. He left behind a note which read, "I've been awake all night. It's terrible."

The house then sat vacant for 46 years.

Unlike many other abandoned estates, the Schweppe Mansion never fell into total decay, but instead continued to be maintained. Over the passing years, the stories began to emerge. Locals, as well as visitors and caretakers, insisted the home was haunted. Apparitions were seen wandering the halls on a consistent basis. The general consensus was the mansion was haunted by the ghosts of both Laura and Charles, as well as several servants.

On one occasion, a caretaker of the estate who had known Charles Schweppe was locking things up for the night when he encountered a man standing silently in the backyard, gazing upward at the house. The man asked how things were at the house, and the caretaker replied that everything was fine. The unexpected figure then walked off. The caretaker would later swear that the man he had spoken with was the late Charles Schweppe.

Note: The Schweppe Mansion was eventually acquired by a couple in the 1980s who painstakingly rehabbed it and occupied it for a period. It's now back on the market.

The Stickney House
1904 Cherry Valley Road, Woodstock, IL 60098

What if I told you that a somewhat-bizarre Woodstock mansion, constructed by spiritualists who regularly conducted séances there to contact the dead, was haunted? What if I threw in the fact the home was built with no 90 degree corners so spirits could roam freely? Hard to believe, right?

George and Sylvia Stickney had this large home built in 1865 to their exact specifications. They were both accomplished mediums who found then-remote Woodstock to be an ideal setting for their forays into the supernatural. They firmly believed in survival after death and conducted countless rituals and activities here to explore spirit communication.

Sylvia was said to have a remarkable gift for speaking with the departed. Friends who shared their interests were regularly invited to participate. Séances were held up in the large second-floor ballroom. The Stickneys had ten children, but only three survived to adulthood. It's believed that the over-riding reason for the séances, at least at first, was to make contact with those who had died.

Befitting the nature of things, even the deaths of George and Sylvia are somewhat mysterious, since they were apparently never well-documented. We do know that George died first, and according to legend, not peacefully. It was said that he was found slumped in a first-floor chair with a look of intense horror on his face.

In the years following his death, the Stickneys's prominence within the spiritualist community continued to grow. Sylvia continued conducting séances, now adding her late husband's spirit to the list of those being contacted.

When Sylvia died, the house began a decline into decay. It lay abandoned for many years, and gained a reputation among locals as being haunted.

In the 1960s, a group of burned-out hippie-types illegally occupied the building for a spell, leaving behind fire damage and graffiti-sprayed walls. Local legend has it that they also conducted black magic rituals, but the claim is unsubstantiated. The home was then purchased by owners hoping to restore it to its former glory, but they moved on when plans fell through.

Eventually, the property was taken over by the Village of Bull Valley. The first floor now houses village offices and a small police department.

Paranormal activity: While current village officials laugh at the rumors of ghostly goings-on, several former employees certainly don't. They have reported hearing a number of strange sounds coming from the notorious second-floor ballroom, now used as a storage area, including ghostly footsteps and human voices. Objects sometimes would move around on desks, doorknobs would turn, lights repeatedly flicked on and off, and doors would open, seemingly of their own volition.

At least one police officer has claimed a direct encounter with an apparition—and two other employees have resigned, citing an inability to handle the paranormal activities within the building.

🔍 *Note:* There are apparently village plans afoot to renovate the ballroom to its original glory, with an overall goal to convert Stickney House into a museum and community center.

Marion Lambert:
The Lonely Ghost of Sheridan Road
Sheridan Road between
Westleigh Road & McCormick Drive
Lake Forest IL 60045

Sheridan Road, which winds through the elegant environs of the Northshore's most prestigious suburb, is a most unlikely place to encounter a ghost standing by the side of the road.

But that's exactly what motorists have reported over the years.

Unlike the far more famous "Resurrection Mary," the ghost of poor Marion Lambert does not dance with young men at local ballrooms, borrow their sweaters, or hitchhike to nearby cemeteries. She simply stands forlornly by the side of Sheridan Road.

Here's the story: In 1916, 17-year-old Marion Lambert lived with her family on the large Lake Forest estate of clothing tycoon Jonas Kuppenheimer. Her father, Frank, was the head caretaker of the property. Marion attended Deerfield Shields High School, where she was a lively and popular student. She had begun a romantic relationship with a local 21-year-old young man, Will Orpet, the son of another Lake Forest caretaker supervising the vast estate of millionaire Cyrus McCormick. By 1916, Orpit was a college junior, attending the University of Wisconsin in Madison.

On visits home, Will pursued Marion relentlessly, and gradually the nature of the relationship changed. Once the young girl gave in to the romantic inclinations of the older boy, he began to lose interest. Where once Orpit appeared infatuated with her, now Marion desperately desired him.

The turn from mere troubled young love to tragedy began when Marion wrote a letter to Orbit, informing him she feared she was pregnant (she really wasn't) and imploring him to return to Lake Forest to discuss the situation in person. An upset Orpit replied, agreeing to return—but instructing Marion to tell no one about it. He assured her that things would be fine; he would take care of everything.

Orpit went to great lengths to cover up his trip back home, including postdating letters to be mailed by a friend in Madison. He took a train to Lake Forest on February 8 and spent the night, unnoticed, in a greenhouse on the McCormick estate. He had previously placed a call to Marion, instructing her to meet him the next morning at Helm Wood, a wooded area close to a nearby train station.

On the morning of February 9, Marion Lambert, having

As shown on the cover: Marion Lambert's ghost has appeared along this stretch of Sheridan Road.

turned 18 three days before, set off with a friend for the Sacred Heart train station, where they routinely caught the train south to Deerfield High School. At the last moment, Marion informed her friend she would not be traveling with her; she claimed she had to mail an important letter at the post office.

Marion had informed her parents she would attend an afterschool party and return that evening on the 8:05 train from Highland Park. Her father waited at the station for her arrival, but she wasn't on the train. She wasn't on the next train, either. Her anxious father then drove south to Highland Park, only to find that not only had she not been at the party, but she hadn't appeared at school that day. A worried and confused Frank Lambert returned home and began a painful vigil.

Before dawn the following morning, Lambert returned to the train station to search for his daughter but could find no traces in the darkness. He left, but soon returned with a neighbor as soon as daylight permitted. They found two sets of footprints in the snow leading away from the station into

the wooded adjacent area known as Helm Wood. They followed the trail into the forest until arriving at a clearing.

Near a cluster of three trees, the body of Marion Lambert
was found. She lay on her side, schoolbooks tucked under her
arm. Her right hand was ungloved and filled with a powdery
white substance. The girl's lips were bloody and blistered as if
burned.

Authorities were immediately notified, and an autopsy
was conducted. The results revealed that the girl had died after
consuming a mixture of arsenic and another acidic substance.
The police, being appraised of the circumstances and after in-
terviewing Marion's family and friends, ordered Will Orpit arrested in Madison. He was soon charged with the murder of
Marion Lambert.

The Trial (May 15, 1916) in a nutshell: The prosecution
claimed that Will Orpit had killed Marion Lambert with poison to avoid marriage. He convinced her to ingest a concoc-
tion he promised would terminate her pregnancy and ensure
that a newly-restored relationship would proceed without the
cloud of dishonor. Orpit, it was pointed out, had easy access
to cyanide at the McCormick greenhouse, where he had spent
the night of February 8. His efforts to conceal his secret trip to
Lake Forest were pointed out.

Orpit and his defense team countered by declaring that
while it was true that he had traveled secretly in from Madison to meet with Marion near the train station on the morning
of the 9th, he knew nothing about any poison. He had only
agreed to the meeting because the girl had threatened suicide.
He claimed that he had gently attempted to break off their
relationship, but wound up arguing with her in the wooded
area for nearly two hours. Marion insisted, said Orpit, that she
would kill herself if he ended the romance. At last, again according to Orpit, he left the area.

The case was ultimately decided by the type of poison
that killed Marion Lambert. It was ultimately proven that the
type that she ingested was potassium cyanide—the type available to Will Orpit in the McCormick greenhouse was sodium
cyanide. But potassium cyanide was readily available in the

science labs at Deerfield High School.

On July 15, 1916, Will Orpit was acquitted and walked out of the courtroom a free man.

The Ghost: Late-night travelers motoring along Sheridan Road on the stretch just north of Westleigh Road have reported seeing the figure of a girl standing forlornly on the eastern side of the road. This area was once known as Helm Wood, and back among the trees south of Westleigh, the body of Marion Lambert had been found that cold February morning in 1916.

The ghostly, translucent figure is described as young and attractive, with short, dark hair. She is clad in a long, blue dress, which appears rain- (or snow-) soaked. Some witnesses have reported that before vanishing, the apparition forms her mouth into a ghastly smile, displaying blistered lips and rotting teeth.

Is Mary Lambert still crying out for justice—or condemned to walk the earth in penance for taking her own life and causing her family such pain?

Marion Lambert Death Site (just behind this home)
550 Rockefeller Road, Lake Forest IL 60045

🖋*Note:* Thanks to the research by the kind folks at the History Center of Lake Forest/Lake Bluff, the exact site where poor Marion Lambert's body was discovered has been identified. Just behind this home, was the small clearing where Frank Lambert discovered the lifeless body of his daughter. The houses here are now private residences, so you can't actually visit the spot, but you can view some of the area from the street.

Ghost Sighting Location
Sheridan Road, just north of Westleigh Road,
Lake Forest IL 60045

Marion Lambert Grave
Lake Forest Cemetery, 1525 Lake Road, Lake Forest IL 60045

2. THE CHICAGO MOB

Al Capone:
Seven Notable Scarface Sites

Newsflash: Al ("Scarface") Capone was Chicago's most famous gangster. Okay, most everyone knows something of him. What most people don't realize is that Big Al was only 26 when he assumed control of a criminal gang here and only 33 years old when he was sent off to prison on tax evasion charges in 1932, thus effectively ending his reign as crime boss of Chicago. Now, if I only had a nickel for every supposed claimed Capone-intense site in the Windy City, I'd be a very rich man.

I don't know how many times I've been advised, "Al hung out here," "This was Al's favorite bar," etc., etc., etc. 97% of these tips turn out to be complete garbage. Capone would have needed to have lived at least 300 years to frequent all the places and cover all the ground quite sincere tipsters solemnly point out.

I'm not going to devote any meaningful time to him, other than to list a few gratuitous sites, well, just because I suspect some people might be somewhat upset if a book at least partly about Chicago gangster stuff fails to include at least a chunk about the notorious Mr. Capone.

The Four Deuces (now long gone)
2222 S. Wabash Avenue, Chicago IL 60616
Big Jim Colosimo was Chicago's first big deal crime lead-

er. He controlled most of the vice activities, including extortion, gambling and prostitution, in the area just south of the Loop known as "The Levee." To aid him, he imported New York gangster Johnny Torrio in 1908, who quickly became his first lieutenant.

Torrio, in turn, sent back to New York for a young Al Capone to serve as an apprentice. Capone was quickly installed primarily as a bouncer at the Four Deuces, a saloon/gambling den/brothel controlled by Colosimo and Torrio on South Wabash Avenue. His expertise impressed Torrio, who quickly made Al his right hand man.

Colosimo's Cafe (now long gone)
2126 S. Wabash Avenue, Chicago IL 60616

Big Jim was a larger-than-life character. His profits from illegal activities had made him very rich. This was not enough to satisfy; he craved the limelight. To that end, he opened a very fancy restaurant, Colosimo's Café, where the powerful, rich and famous wined and dined, and it was said he actually lost money in trying to impress.

Colosimo soon fell behind the times. The advent of Prohibition in 1920 created a golden profit opportunity for mobsters in Chicago, but Big Jim had no interest, preferring to now primarily occupy himself with entertaining at his café with a new young wife and playing the role of magnanimous bigshot. This rankled his #2, Johnny Torrio, to no end.

The budding liquor rackets beckoned; unbelievable profits were there for the taking. Matters came to a head: Torrio decided that Colosimo had to go.

Big Jim was gunned down by an assassin at his café on May 11, 1920. The murder has remained unsolved to this day. Certainly the man with the clearest motive for wanting Big Jim gone was Torrio, who quickly ascended into the leadership role in the Colosimo empire—but there was a good chance the actual triggerman was his protégé, young Alphonse Capone.

Note: The building is gone—just an empty lot now.

Al Capone's Chicago Headquarters
Metropole Hotel (now demolished)
2300 S. Michigan Avenue, Chicago IL 60616
Lexingtom Hotel (now demolished)
2135 S. Michigan Avenue, Chicago IL 60616

Actually, Capone had two headquarters in Chicago: the Metropole Hotel, which he used from 1925 to 1928, and the Lexington Hotel, used from 1928 to 1931. At the Lexington, Geraldo Rivera broadcast his notoriously comic 1986 search for the "hidden vaults of Al Capone," which of course found nothing.

Al Capone's Home (the neighborhood was fancier then.)
7244 S. Prairie Avenue, Chicago IL 60619

Al lived here, or at least it was considered his primary Chicago residence from 1923 onward. He did spend a lot of time at his Florida estate. Even after he passed away in Florida in 1947, the home remained in Capone family hands until 1953, when it was sold to outsiders.

The home, still standing, is really nothing special to look at; hardly what you might expect from a man who was the virtual king of Chicago.

The Klas Restaurant (Al Capone actually did eat here.)
5734 N. Cermak (22nd Street) Cicero IL 60804

This actually was a place Big Al visited regularly. I imagine that pork shanks and liver dumplings (it was a Bohemian-style place) served as an occasional welcome alternative to the steady stream of pasta he regularly dealt with.

Note: After many years, The Klas closed. As of July 2019, the property was listed for sale. The façade of the building is very cool, although run down quite a bit.

Al Capone's Funeral: Rago Brothers Funeral Home
621 N. Western Avenue, Chicago IL 60612

Big Al died on January 25, 1947, in Miami Beach, Florida, his brain ravaged by the effects of late-stage syphilis. His

The Klas Restaurant in Berwyn. Al Capone really did dine here.

funeral was held here on February 4. It is said that another empty coffin was sent from Miami Beach elsewhere to throw reporters off the track.

Note: The funeral of fellow gangster "Machine Gun" Jack McGurn had also taken place here in 1936.

No look at Al Capone could ignore the Chicago crime event most closely associated with him, so here we go:

The St. Valentine's Day Massacre

I have to admit that all of the "Gangster Tour" buses do visit this site. Strike one.

And yes, I know, I know, I made a big deal in the introduction about not bothering with a long section about it. Strike two.

But … I do have a few site recommendations connected to the Massacre—and to fully appreciate them, I feel it appropriate to provide a little backdrop.

The St. Valentine's Day Massacre in a nutshell:

1. During the Prohibition years, gangsters fought a bloody war to control the illegal booze trade in Chicago.

2. The two main combatants: The Northside gang, led by a succession of leaders, and the Southside gang, most notably led by Al Capone.

3. The Valentine's Day Massacre didn't just happen. There were many, many instances of attacks and reprisals between the two gangs that led to it.

4. Things went back and forth. A double-cross (involving the sale of a brewery) of Southside chief Johnny Torrio by Northside leader Dion O'Banion led to O'Banion getting gunned down in his flower shop/headquarters, known as Schofield's.

In revenge, Torrio was severely wounded in a hit attempt, causing him to retire and hand the reins over to a young Al Capone. Capone soon went after the new Northside leader, Hymie Weiss, who was fatally machinegun-ambushed in the street between Schofield's and Holy Name Cathedral.

In addition, another member of the gang, Vincent "The Schemer" Drucci was killed by a policeman while (supposedly) resisting arrest in 1927. Just prior to the St. Valentine's Day Massacre, another Capone crony, Patsy Lolordo, was murdered in his home in a hit orchestrated by Bugs Moran.

5. By 1929, George "Bugs" Moran was the Northside leader.

6. Capone (supposedly) grew weary of the constant strife, especially after a convoy of Northsider cars machine gun strafed a restaurant where he was dining, and decided to eliminate the rival gang in one fell swoop.

7. Two of Capone's men dressed in police uniforms, along with two others pretending to be plainclothes cops, paid a visit February 14, 1929, to the SMC Cartage Company—in reality, the rival gang's headquarters. Unbeknownst to them, Bugs was not there.

8. Thinking it just another typical police raid, the seven Moran gang members present dutifully lined up facing a brick wall. The bogus cops produced machine guns and shotguns and massacred all seven before leaving the scene in their getaway car.

9. This brutal crime finally turned the tide of public opinion against Al Capone, who, up till that time, was viewed as a kind of Robin Hood by many Chicagoans.

The St. Valentine's Day Massacre Site
2122 N. Clark St., Chicago IL 60614

Formerly the site of the SMC Cartage Co. Nothing is left of it now; it's just an empty-ish little lot. No plaque, no nothing. The only remaining tie here to the crime is the building on the opposite side of Clark (the now-home of the Chicago Pizza and Oven Grinder restaurant), which was used as a lookout post by the Capone gang.

Okay, on to the other sites connected to the Massacre:

Where the Getaway Car was Found
1723 N. Wood St. Chicago IL 60622 (garage in alley)

On February 21, a week after the Massacre, police, following a tip, discovered the remains of a black 1927 Cadillac in a garage here. In an obvious attempt to destroy evidence, it had been both chopped up and burned.

Note: I have heard that the garage standing here now replaced the original, but it does look pretty old.

Did Bugs Moran Hide Here?
Clark St. & Dickens Avenue, Chicago IL 60614

Okay, this one might be pure speculation, and I freely admit it. There's no evidence whatsoever. But: Bugs Moran just may have narrowly missed death on that Valentine's Day by being late to his headquarters at 2122 N. Clark.

As the story goes, he was on his way when he saw police activity at the SMC Cartage Company. He ducked into a nearby diner and waited things out.

Now, where was that diner? Not all that long ago, there was a small coffee shop on the northwest corner of this intersection. A few older neighborhood guys I know pointed it out as the place. As I've said, I can't verify it. Just sayin'.

Peter ("Goosey") and Frank ("Hock") Gusenberg: Two Notable Victims
437 Roscoe, Chicago IL 60657 (where they grew up)

Pete and brother Frank Gusenberg were, without a doubt, the scariest members of Bugs Moran's Northside gang. They functioned as the gang's enforcers. Pete was said to have calmly emptied an entire machine gun magazine at the Hawthorne Restaurant in Cicero in the attempt to whack Al Capone. Frank was there, too. They both also made several unsuccessful attempts to kill Capone's lieutenant Machine Gun Jack McGurn.

The brothers were two of the St. Valentine's Day seven victims. Frank was actually still (barely) alive when police arrived at the SMC Cartage site. He was quickly whisked off to a hospital.

When asked there who had shot him, he replied, "No one shot me."

Then he died.

Drake-Braithwaite Co.: Remains of the Day
2219 -21 Lincoln Avenue, Chicago IL 60614

Six of the seven victims were brought here by police on orders from the Cook County coroner.

Note: The building still stands, but it's no longer a funeral home.

Gusenberg Graves
Irving Park Cemetery (Bethayers Section)
7777 W. Irving Park Road, Chicago IL 60634

The Lead Up—Sites connected to the St. Valentine's Day Massacre:

As mentioned previously, the St. Valentine's Day Massacre was really a kind of bloody culmination of years of hostility between the North and South side gangs. Here are several relevant sites:

Schofield Flower Shop
(Dion O'Banion and Hymie Weiss got it here)
738 N. State Street, Chicago IL 60654
(across the street from Holy Name Cathedral)
Tour buses do go here, so we won't dwell—other than to mention that two Northside Gang leaders, whose actions led inexorably to the St. Valentine's Day Massacre, were fatally ambushed here at different times: Dion O'Banion, inside the shop on November 19, 1924, and Hymie Weiss, in the street just outside on October 11, 1926. The building is long gone, anyway.

Hawthorne Hotel:
(the Ambush that Got Al Capone really angry)
4823 W. 22nd Street (Cermak Road), Cicero IL 60804
The Northside gang held Al Capone directly responsible for the hit on their chief, Dion O'Banion, in November of 1924, and swore revenge. They patiently plotted.

On September 20, 1926, Al was having lunch at this hotel restaurant when a car slowly rolled down 22nd Street. Suddenly, the sound of gunfire erupted. Capone's bodyguard (reportedly a young hood named Tony Accardo, who we will meet later) dragged him to the floor and out of range. Once the firing stopped, Capone rose and ran to the door to view the assailants. He suddenly noticed that nothing had been damaged in the restaurant; the bullets had been blanks.

At that moment, a convoy of six more cars, containing new Northside gang boss Hymie Weis and the notorious Gusenberg brothers, showed up and blasted away with machine guns—and this time the bullets were not blanks. Again, Capone hit the deck.

It's pretty remarkable that despite over 1,000 rounds of ammunition being blasted into the hotel, no one was killed.

Al Capone's Hawthorne Hotel once stood here. On September 20, 1926, a rival gang poured over 1,000 machine gun rounds into it in an attempt to assassinate Scarface.

Al Capone decided here, at the Hawthorne, that enough was enough. He would soon have his revenge on Hymie Weiss.

Note: Today, the Hawthorne is gone. The site is now a bank parking lot.

Hymie Weiss Sites
(the man whom even Capone feared)

Hymie Weiss (real name Henry Earl Wojciechowski) was said to be the only man Al Capone feared. And, especially after the Hawthorne Hotel attack, he was most certainly a very large stone in Capone's shoe.

With the death of Dion O'Banion, Weiss assumed control of the Northside gang. And he was out for revenge. When Al Capone arranged a meeting in an effort to make peace (Big Al sent an emissary; it was said that Weiss' stare gave him the shivers), Weiss refused and stormed out. No peace talks would be possible until Capone handed over two of the men Weiss was convinced had murdered his boss, O'Banion.

Capone decided no peace would ever really be possible with the volatile Weiss, and began plotting the hit that would soon take place near the Schofield Flower Shop.

Hymie Weiss Home. 3808 W. Grand Avenue, Chicago IL 60651.

🔍*Note:* Weiss lived here as a youth. His dad ran a nearby saloon. The house is still there.

P.S.: Hymie Weiss is credited by many crime historians as coining the infamous mob phrase, "Take him for a ride."

Hymie Weiss Grave: Mount Carmel Catholic Cemetery. 1400 S. Wolf Road, Hillside IL 60162 (Section K, Block 4).

The Patsy Lolordo Murder: A Respectful Hit
1921 W. North Avenue, Chicago IL 60622 (top floor)

Pasquelino ("Patsy") Lolordo was the newly-installed head of Chicago's Unione Siciliano, ostensibly a fraternal and social welfare organization, but really a puppet organization of the mob, and especially Al Capone. His immediate predecessor, Tony Lombardo (also a Capone confederate), had been assassinated near the Chicago intersection of Madison and Dearborn the previous September. No one had been charged in the crime.

Both Lolordo and Lombardo had drawn the wrath of another Chicago Italian gangster, Joe Aiello, who wanted to control the Unione himself. He saw the ascension of these two Capone allies as threatening to his own interests. His resentment over Capone's growing power drove him into an unlikely alliance with another Capone enemy, Bugs Moran.

On January 8, 1929, only months into his leadership stint (and a month before the St. Valentine's Day Massacre), Lolordo was visited at his home here by three men claiming to seek his counsel. He suspected nothing. With his wife and a housemaid busily occupied doing chores in the kitchen, his visitors suddenly produced handguns and pumped bullets in him.

Before their quick departure, they placed a pillow beneath Lolordo's head. Whether this was meant as a sign of respect or contempt is unknown. It is thought that Joe Aiello and Bugs Moran were the driving forces behind the murder, but no formal charges were ever brought.

Note: The building is still there, with the lower floor now occupied by an orthodontist's office.

The Joe Aiello Murder: Capone's Post-Massacre Revenge
205 N. Kolmar, Chicago IL 60624
Even after the St. Valentine's Day Massacre virtually eliminated his main threat, the Northside gang, Al Capone was not yet done. Joe Aiello, who Capone held responsible for the deaths of allies Lolordo and Lombardo, as well as for attacks on both himself and key lieutenants, had to go.

Capone ordered a lethal machine gun attack on Aiello as he left this location, where he had been hiding out, on October 23, 1930.

Note: The house remains.

Outfit Bigshots *not* Named Capone

The "Outfit," of course, is the charming Chicago sobriquet for the local Mob/Mafia/La Cosa Nostra conglomerate that has remained a shadowy presence in the Windy City since forever. Gone now are the constant gang wars that raged in the period when Al Capone's Southside crew battled the Dean O'Banion/ Hymie Weiss/Bugs Moran Northsiders for control of the city's lucrative booze traffic; that pretty much ended with the St. Valentine's Day Massacre of 1929.

But no matter how much things change, like the return of legal hootch with the repeal of the 19th Amendment, the Outfit always seems to stand ready to adapt and survive. Even somewhat questionable changes in leadership, not all particularly successful in the years following the Capone reign, failed to stop the Chicago Mob. (Al was hauled off to prison on tax charges in 1932 and would never control Chicago again).

The leaders who followed Capone, including Frank "The Enforcer" Nitti, Paul "The Waiter" Ricca, Jack "Machine Gun" McGurn, Tony "Big Tuna" Accardo, Sam "Momo" Giancana and Tony "The Ant" Spilotro, seemed to heed Horace Greeley's advice and looked west for their homes.

The suburbs to the west of Chicago, most notably River Forest and Oak Park, seemed to draw them like flies. It was said for many years that these areas were about as safe as it gets in Chicago. The crime bosses insisted upon keeping their own areas pristine. Those who dared disobey did so at their peril. These guys didn't mess around.

The names to know:

Tony Accardo: The Real Godfather

Al Capone? Al CaPONE? Fuggetabotim! How about the man it was said "had more brains before breakfast than Al Capone had all day?"

Tony Accardo was a far more erudite leader of the Outfit, a true Chicago Godfather. He ruled the roost full-time from 1943 to 1957, and would continue to serve as kind of "chairman" probably right up until his death.

No matter who was thought by the authorities to be in charge of the Outfit, it was always Tony Accardo actually pulling the strings behind the scene. Virtually no major decisions could be made without clearing it with him. Not only did he exert a major influence on politics, business, vice and, well— everything in town, he operated in true old-school Mafiosi fashion, always under the radar, skillfully exerting his vast powers behind the scenes, and avoiding calling attention to himself whenever possible. In other words, the virtual antithesis of the showy Scarface Al.

How successful was this approach? Under his leadership, the Outfit grew into an even more wildly profitable organization, extending its insidious tentacles beyond the usual illegal activities into legitimate businesses as well. And Accardo, unlike virtually every other high-profile Mafia boss, never spent a night in jail, and wound up dying of natural causes in 1992.

Pretty impressive.

I've always admired Tony's two most famous nicknames, which were kind of cool even for mobster nicknames. It was said that it was Capone himself, who Accardo had begun assisting in the 20s, assigned him the charming moniker "Joe Batters," allegedly for his prowess with a baseball bat (a very useful skill to have on your gangster resume). A point of interest here: in 1929, Albert Anselmi and John Scalise, two Capone gunmen suspected by Capone of plotting against him, were lured to what was supposedly a dinner in their honor. Their after-dinner reward? It is said that they were bludgeoned to death with a Louisville Slugger (and shot, too) before being ignominiously dumped by a roadside in Hammond, Indiana.

I've always wondered if this was Accardo's tryout audition for the Outfit big leagues.

Tony's other notable nickname was "Big Tuna." This one doesn't have as interesting of a backstory (it supposedly memorialized a very large fish he caught in Florida), but it still has kind of a cool ring. Imagine the conversation in some murky South Wabash dive:

Voice 1: "Let's just whack that guy! I gotta get rid o dat stone in my shoe!"

Voice 2: "Hold on dere, buddy boy—you know we can't do dat widout checking it out first wid da Big Tuna."

Even later in life and for all of his legendary cautious restraint, Accardo could, however, be provoked back into displaying the rage and vindictiveness that marked his early career.

On January 6, 1978, several disgruntled thieves made the astoundingly ill thought out decision to burgle his River Forest home. I still marvel at how bone-headed it would be to pick—of all possible places—the home of the Outfit's boss to rob. Sometimes, all you can do is shake your head.

Accardo, on vacation at the time, was notified. He flew home immediately.

Within nine days of the burglary, the heads began to roll. Before long, ten people suspected of being in on the heist were found murdered in gruesome fashion all over Chicago. Even the Accardo butler (I guess no one was above suspicion) vanished, never to be seen again.

Some kind of Godfather! Some kind of Big Tuna!

Notable Tony Accardo Sites:

Tony's First House. 915 Franklin Avenue, River Forest IL 60305. This is a real palace; exactly the kind of mansion you would have if you were a Mob boss. Big, huge, gigantic. Twenty-two rooms. Nine bedrooms, plus an indoor swimming pool and bowling alley. Accardo lived here from 1951 to 1963 until his better instincts kicked in, probably realizing that the uber-ostentatious home was the equivalent of waving a red flag in the faces of the IRS bulls. After all, how could a guy claiming to be a beer salesman afford the Taj Mahal?

Tony's Second House. 1407 Ashland Avenue, River Forest IL 60305. This ranch home, not far from his first one, is a lot more modest. A lot. In fact, this house is pretty much like one you might expect a moderately successful beer salesman to own.

This is the home that was robbed by the nutballs.

Meo's Norwood House: The Big Tuna's Restaurant of Choice. 4750 N. Harlem Avenue, Harwood Heights IL 60706. Accardo frequently dined with his shady associates at this Harwood Heights Restaurant, then known as Meo's Norwood House. It was famous for staging "fashion/lingerie shows" for the local Good Fellas. Countless mob business decisions were decided here, as well as the fates of many wiseguys.

The establishment later changed hands, becoming the Old Warsaw Inn, and became much more of a family-oriented place. I guess they had to give up on those lingerie shows.

Note: As of February 2019, the Old Warsaw closed its doors and the entire structure has been demolished. It looks like something new will soon occupy the site.

Sam Giancana: They Always Send Someone You Trust

First of all, I don't find Sam's Mob nicknames—"Momo," "Mooney," and "The Weasel"—at all interesting. Momo? Boring. Mooney? Dull. The Weasel? Just look up a photo of the guy online. Subject closed.

By most accounts, Giancana was a pretty crummy guy, mean-tempered, unpleasant, and always craving the spotlight. He (kind of) took over (his actual title is somewhat under debate) from Tony Accardo in 1957, and held a lot of sway in Chicago until 1965. During this period, he was said to have swung Illinois votes in the 1960 presidential race to Senator John Kennedy, ensuring the JFK victory, participated in a plan with the CIA to assassinate Fidel Castro (and how did that work out?), wooed popular singer Phyliss McGuire of The McGuire Sisters, and of course, functioned as the official idol of notorious Wise Guy fan Frank Sinatra.

Oh, almost forgot: he was rumored to have been involved in the plot to assassinate JFK.

Of course.

Giancana was a graduate of the juvenile 42 Gang, which was formed in the Italian neighborhoods on the West Side and terrorized surrounding areas. This gang awarded particularly colorful hood nicknames to their members (except Sam). Some especially interesting ones: "Willie Potatoes" Daddano, "Milwaukee Phil" Alderisio, "Cockeyed Louie" Fratto, "Mad Sam" DeStefano, and the pungently expressive "Teets" Battaglia.

Sam paid his dues, learned his larcenous trade, and was soon promoted to the Outfit, where he quickly climbed the leadership ladder. He caught the attention of boss Tony Accardo when he proposed a plan to take over the numbers racket in the black neighborhoods of Chicago.

This enterprise proved extremely profitable and enhanced Giancana's status as a valuable mob earner.

In 1957, Chicago boss Tony Accardo decided to semi-retire and hand over the day-to-day Outfit supervising role to Giancana. Still, Accardo remained the real Outfit power; all important decisions had to be run by him before being implemented.

Nevertheless, it was Giancana who was (allegedly) contacted by Kennedy Family patriarch Joe Kennedy for help during his son John's 1960 presidential campaign. Whether this is true or not, it is a fact that Illinois' electoral win for JFK ensured a narrow victory over Richard Nixon.

The Outfit expected that Kennedy would return the favor by going easy on them while in the White House. In fact, just the reverse happened; JFK's Attorney General, brother Robert Kennedy, proved a zealous opponent. Mob leadership was outraged by this seeming betrayal and vowed revenge. It has long been thought by many that the Mafia played a key role in Kennedy's 1963 assassination.

It was also in the early 60s that Giancana was approached by the CIA for help in planning an assassination attempt on Cuban leader Fidel Castro, which was unsuccessful.

Sam Giancana by now was beginning to flirt a bit dangerously with Outfit Etiquette 101: keep a low profile. He was being drawn to the limelight, socializing openly with entertainment stars like Frank Sinatra and Marilyn Monroe and conducting a very high-profile affair with singer Phyliss McGuire. This did not sit well with other higher-ups in Chicago, who were beginning to feel that Momo's attention was no longer on mob business.

When Giancana was called in 1966 to testify before a grand jury investigating organized crime activities, he was ordered by Outfit hierarchy (read: Tony Accardo) to remain silent. He did just that and received a year in jail for his refusal to cooperate. While he was serving his sentence, Accardo, tired of his performance, replaced him as the day-to-day boss.

When Giancana emerged from prison, he found that he was now persona non grata in Chicago. He left for Mexico, where he quickly began establishing a successful gambling empire that operated in a number of countries across the world. Word soon arrived from Chicago that Tony Accardo was demanding a cut from Sam's new enterprise. Giancana angrily refused, claiming that since he now had no ties with the Outfit, he had no obligation to kick back any proceeds. This, of course, did not sit well with Accardo.

By 1974, Giancana had worn out his welcome in Mexico and returned to Chicago. He was scheduled to appear soon before a US Senate committee investigating mob involvement with the failed plan to assassinate Cuba's Fidel Castro. And he was still refusing to share his gambling profits with the Outfit.

On the night of June 19, 1974, Giancana was preparing a meal in the basement kitchen of his Oak Park home. He had a visitor, without doubt someone he trusted. As he leaned over the stove, this trusted guest approached from behind and put a .22 caliber bullet into the back of his head. For good measure, the killer put six more slugs through his chin as a mob message about the dangers of even considering talking to the Feds. The assassin then exited the residence back into the night.

I've always wondered if he whispered to himself, "Leave the sausage. Take the gun."

There were plenty of people who wanted Sam Giancana dead, but the case remains unsolved.

Sam Giancana's Home/Murder Site). 1147 Wenonah Avenue, Oak Park IL 60304. Giancana's life ended in the basement.

🔑 *Note:* the Spilotro home (the Spilotro brothers will be covered shortly) is only a short walk away.

Armory Lounge: Giancana's Unofficial Headquarters. 7427 Roosevelt Road, Forest Park IL 60130. Giancana conducted a lot of Outfit business here. The Armory would eventually be successfully bugged, and provide authorities with a wealth of information on mob activities.

🔑 *Note:* It's no longer the Armory; as of 2019, it's known as "Charlies."

Giancana's Funeral: MontClair Lucania Funeral Home. 6901 W. Belmont Avenue, Chicago, IL 60634.

 Bonus:

Sam Giancana's Last Meal/ Dine Like a Mafioso

Giancana was preparing an Italian favorite, sausage, escarole and beans, when he was whacked.
Here's the recipe:

Ingredients
- 1 lb. Italian sausage
- 3 tbls. olive oil
- 3 garlic cloves
- 1 bunch escarole (or spinach)
- 1 can Great Northern beans
- 1 chili pepper
- 4 tbls. dry white wine
- grated Romano or Parmesan cheese

Preparation: Brown the sausage in the olive oil. Remove sausage, saute garlic. Return sausage to pan, add beans (with juice). Cook on medium-high heat for five minutes. Add escarole, lower temperature to medium-low. Cook ten minutes. Add diced chili pepper and wine. Simmer on low for five minutes. Serve with grated cheese.

P.S: Don't allow anyone to sidle up behind you.

Jack McGurn, aka "Machine Gun" Jack
Capone's Ace Triggerman

Now what was a nice Irish guy doing in Capone's Italian cutthroat gang, you might ask?

Well, good question. Here's the answer: Jack McGurn was really one Vincenzo Antonio Gibaldi. Now I can understand why he changed it. Machine Gun Jack McGurn has a much more mobby ring to it. Vincenzo Antonio Gibaldi sounds like the name of some obscure Italian tragic poet, unread now for 500 years or so.

Jack grew up in the Little Sicily neighborhood on Chicago's West Side. He tried his hand at boxing, billing himself

"Machine Gun" Jack McGurn was whacked at this former bowling alley on February 15, 1936.

as "Battling Jack McGurn," and had some success. He would soon find his true calling, however, by joining a larcenous group known as the "Circus Gang" (based in a North Avenue dive called The Circus Café).

Jack's fellow gang members included such luminaries as Claude "Screwy" Maddox, "Tough Tony" Capezio, and soon, a young Tony Accardo (who had yet to be awarded a colorful sobriquet).

McGurn quickly came to the notice of Al Capone (who was said to have greatly admired Jack's physical fitness training routines, as well as his weaponry skills), and soon became one of Big Al's most trusted lieutenants. When Capone began to desperately need to bring new gang recruits on board to manage his burgeoning criminal empire, he turned to McGurn for advice. One of the first names Jack suggested was Tony Accardo.

McGurn had his finger in a lot of Windy City activities,

both legal and illegal. He was a part owner of the famous Green Mill Lounge, which still stands today in Uptown. When famous (for the time) singer/comedian Joe E. Brown left his Green Mill gig for a higher paying job at another nearby joint (controlled by a rival mob), Jack had him pistol-whipped and throat-slashed (he did manage to recover). Machine Gun, as his name implied, was not a man to cross.

The most famous Chicago gangland event of all time, of course, was The St. Valentine's Day Massacre (more on it later), and if we accept the commonly-held theory that holds Capone guilty of it, then surely Machine Gun Jack McGurn had to be a key player (he was very smart, and regarded as a great planner, to boot). The cops thought so, too, but when they collared Jack, he claimed he had spent the entire day of February 14 in bed in room 1919A of the Stevens Hotel with girlfriend/soon-to-be-wife Louise Rolfe.

McGurn certainly had his day in the Chicago Outfit sun, but after Al Capone, his biggest fan, was hauled away to the pen in 1932, his star quickly began to fade.

By 1936, Louise was long gone, he was out of favor with the new mob leadership, and nearly broke. He allegedly began making some very negative comments about his old Outfit pals, which is never a very good idea, and to make things even hairier for him, there were still plenty of hoods around from other gangs who held a variety of grudges.

On February 15, 1936, one day after the seventh anniversary of the St. Valentine's Day Massacre, he was bowling with two pals at the Avenue Recreation Bowling Alley on Milwaukee Avenue. Three men suddenly appeared, and put several bullets into him. For dramatic effect, they placed a comic Valentine's Day card at his feet:

> "You've lost your job, you've lost your dough,
> Your jewels and cars and fancy houses,
> But things could still be worse, you know …
> At least you haven't lost your trousas!"

Notable Machine Gun Jack McGurn Sites:

The Green Mill Lounge (Jack was part owner). 4801 N. Broadway, Chicago IL 60640.

⌕ *Note:* Still here and still worth a visit.

The Commonwealth Hotel (where singer Joe E. Brown was attacked). 2757 Pine Grove Avenue, Chicago IL 60614 (Room 332).

⌕ *Note:* Still there.

The Stevens Hotel (Jack's Blonde Alibi). 720 S. Michigan Avenue, Chicago IL 60605 (Room 1919A).

⌕ *Note:* It's now a Hilton. Louise Rolfe claimed that she and Jack spent February 14 snuggling in room 1919A.

The Avenue Recreation Bowling Alley (where Jack was whacked). 805 N. Milwaukee Avenue, Chicago IL 60642 (2nd floor).

⌕ *Note:* The building is no longer a bowling alley. It has been subdivided into offices.

McGurn Homes. 1114 N. Kenilworth, Oak Park IL 60302 and 1224 N. Kenilworth, Oak Park IL 60302.

⌕ *Note:* Both homes remain.

Frank Nitti, Capone's Successor: A Self-Inflicted Hit

Frank "The Enforcer" Nitti was the number-two man in the Chicago Outfit under Al Capone. He stepped into the leadership role shortly after Capone was sent to prison on income tax charges in 1932.

Nitti was, by all accounts, a very effective mob administrator, extending the Outfit's influence beyond the usual vice activities into labor union control—which lead seamlessly into the extortion of major legitimate industries.

Nitti's downfall came in 1943 when he was indicted for his role in the extortion of Hollywood film studios. Several

Mob boss Frank Nitti committed suicide along a railroad track here in North Riverside on March 19, 1943.

other top Outfit wiseguys were also in trouble over the matter, and they blamed him for dragging them into it.

By March, Nitti was facing three huge problems:

1. He was in trouble with his own organization.
2. He was suffering from cancer.
3. He was facing a long prison sentence (and he was severely claustrophobic).

On March 19, 1943, one day before his scheduled appearance before a grand jury, Nitti fortified himself with a generous amount of alcohol and informed his wife that he was going for a walk. He traveled north for about five blocks to a rail yard.

Several shocked workers nearby observed Nitti produce a .32 caliber revolver and place it to his head. He was either really drunk or really nervous because the first two shots failed to accomplish the mission. The third did, however.

Frank Nitti was the only known mob boss to commit suicide.

Frank Nitti's Home. 712 Selborne Rd, Riverside IL 60546. After previously meeting with other Outfit bosses, Nitti decided it was all over. He bundled up and headed north to the rail yard where he committed suicide.

Note: The home still stands.

Nitti's Death Site. 7501 W. Cermak Road, North Riverside IL 60546. This one's a bit tricky. Park in the North Riverside Park Mall parking lot, then find the abandoned railroad track line to the east (the line runs north/south; the actual tracks are gone). When you see a Hobby Lobby on the east side of the track line, you are in the right place.

Sam DeStefano aka "Mad Sam:" Psychopath Extraordinaire 1656 N. Sayre Avenue, Chicago IL 60707

"Mad Sam" DeStefano was a total whackjob hood, and I've always been surprised he lasted as long as he did with the Outfit. In an environment dominated by extremely violent and often psychopathic men, he was head and shoulders above the herd. To really get a full appreciation of the man, I suggest you take a few moments here to look up some of his highlight moments on the web. They are available. You almost have to, otherwise you will think I completely made him up.

DeStefano was involved in criminal activities from a young age, and became a member of the notorious 42 Gang on the West Side. He became close there with Sam Giancana, a future Chicago boss. His younger years were marked from stints in jail on a variety of charges, including bootlegging, gambling, burglary and rape. During one of his prison stays, he befriended Paul "The Waiter" Ricca, another future Outfit leader.

DeStefano seemed to finally find his true criminal forte as a mob loan shark in the 1950s, in large part because of the fear he inspired with his clients.

To describe his personality and exploits would require many pages, so I've decided that the best way to give you an idea is to simply tick off some of the most illustrative bits:

• DeStefano enjoyed inflicting pain on any who drew his displeasure. His was a master of the icepick and the blowtorch.

• It was said that he often didn't mind if a client couldn't pay up a debt; it supplied an excuse for torturing another human being.

• He actually had a soundproof torture chamber built in the basement of his home.

• Mad Sam was a poster boy for the bipolar personality years before the term came into vogue. Associates claimed that he could go from a joyfully gregarious state to a snarling, drooling meltdown in seconds.

• Those associates also state that he would pray openly to the devil.

• He would often claim if things had only a worked out a bit differently, he would have become President of the United States.

• In 1955, Sam killed a younger brother, Michael, on orders from mob leaders. Michael had become a heroin addict, was gay, and seen as a liability. Sam washed Michael's body and dressed him in a fresh suit before anonymously notifying cops where his body could be found.

• Tony Spilotro (profiled next) would become DeStefano's protégé, and "The Ant" would soon prove invaluable in applying Mad Sam's violent loan repayment techniques.

• When, in 1961, DeStefano suspected an associate named William "Action" Jackson of betrayal, he had Jackson taken to a south side meat-rendering plant. There, Jackson was hoisted up on a meat hook and Sam went to work. When police later discovered his body, they found the man's kneecaps were smashed, he had been stabbed and shot, and had both a cattle prod and a blowtorch applied to his body. He likely endured this treatment for three days before dying from the pain.

• Not even family members were spared from DeStefano's sadistic streak. He once punished his wife for some infraction by kidnapping a stranger and forcing the man to have sex with her.

• DeStefano said he often dreamed about owning a pig

farm where he could feed his victims to the swine.

• When being interviewed by authorities in his home, he would often serve them coffee he had urinated in. He would also parade around with his pants unzipped.

• In 1963, an associate named Leo Foreman drew DeStefano's wrath by kicking him out of his office during a heated argument. Mad Sam had Foreman brought to his basement torture chamber, where the man was murdered—beaten with hammers and stabbed with an icepick.

• As time went on, DeStefano's antics became harder for Outfit leaders to tolerate, since they violated the basic mob tenet of keeping a low profile. A particular tendency really drew their ire: DeStefano, insisting on presenting his own defense in legal matters, would sometimes have himself carried into court dressed in pajamas and shouting from a bullhorn. By 1973, when a former associate-turned-government-witness implicated DeStefano in the Leo Foreman murder ten years before, Mad Sam insisted on continuing this bizarre behavior.

At last, the Chicago bosses decided enough was enough: Mad Sam had to go. His erratic behavior, and the embarrassment it brought, plus the very real possibility that his antics could jeopardize them in other trials, had finally trumped his considerable power as an earner. The word was given to his underlings.

On April 14, 1973, Sam DeStefano waited impatiently in the garage of his home for the arrival of two associates. Ostensibly, they were meeting to discuss plans to eliminate the witness in the upcoming Leo Foreman murder trial. If he were out of the way, the case against DeStefano would collapse.

The meeting didn't go quite as Sam had anticipated. The two associates (widely believed to have been protégé Tony Spilotro* and Sam's own brother, Mario) arrived at the garage. Spilotro produced a shotgun. The first blast hit Sam in the upper chest, tearing off his left arm. Just to be sure, the killer(s) applied a coup de grace shot before fleeing.

Today: the house—and the infamous garage—are still there and look pretty much as they did in 1973.

🔎 *Note:* *I've never been quite convinced that Tony Spilotro was the triggerman here. By 1973, he was already running the show for the Outfit in Las Vegas (as I'll outline in the next section).

So either he flew back to Chicago just to perform this deed *or* it was someone else. Since the name "Spilotro" has long been connected to DeStefano's murder—*and* because The Ant's kid brother, Michael, was a dedicated Tony wannabee—*and* since Michael owned a restaurant at the time only one block south from DeStefano's home, I've always had a nagging suspicion that this hit may have served as the "making his bones" mob initiation of young Michael Spilotro.

Tony Spilotro: An Outfit Cautionary Tale

Do you remember Nicky Santoro, that sawed-off powderkeg hood Joe Peschi portrayed in the film *Casino*? You know, the mob Las Vegas enforcer who winds up angering his bosses and getting beaten to death and buried in a cornfield? That character was based on Outfit enforcer Tony "The Ant" (he stood 5'2") Spilotro.

Spilotro was born in Chicago in 1938, one of six children.

Tony "The Ant" Spilotro's funeral was held here.

His father, Pasquale, owned a restaurant near the Grand Avenue/Ogden intersection, the heart of the Italian neighborhood known as "The Patch." This restaurant was popular with local wiseguys (the meatball sandwich was a favorite with them) and it was here that Tony probably first began to admire the elevated status of the mob-connected.

Tony began having brushes with the law from an early age. He also had a knack for violence. This brought him to the attention of Mad Sam DeStefano, who took him on as a protégé in his loan shark operation. Now DeStefano, as you recall, had a proclivity for violent methods of ensuring his clients paid up on time. Undoubtedly, Spilotro learned a few new tricks at the feet of the psychopathic master. He began to excel at the art of violence.

An example? In 1962, Spilotro was given the task of eliminating a pair of thieves who had drawn Outfit disfavor. He extracted information from one (before slitting his throat) by placing his head in a vise and tightening it until an eyeball burst from his skull.

Spilotro was given the order from mob leaders in 1973 to whack his mentor, Mad Sam, who had fallen out of favor, and this he did with little hesitation. This act seemed to cement his status as a genuine Outfit up-and-comer. He hit the big time when chosen to oversee Chicago mob interests in Las Vegas. There, he was to work in tandem with an old Chicago friend, Frank "Lefty" Rosenthal, a gambler extraordinaire now running casinos—and supervising the "skim," in which casino profits were surreptitiously siphoned off and sent back to the Outfit.

The move to Las Vegas, and the prestige of his new mob status, should have put Spilotro on top of the world. Instead, it was really the beginning of his downfall. From the moment he arrived in Nevada, his temper, inflated sense of importance and heavy-handed leadership style began to negatively impact normally smooth-running Outfit operations.

The Chicago bosses had always attempted to make Las Vegas a relatively violence-free gambling mecca, but suddenly, more murders were being committed than ever before as Spilotro cracked the whip on those displeasing him. His flaunting of local authority would soon see him banned from the very casinos he was supposed to be overseeing.

Things got even worse. Spilotro, not satisfied with the vast sums he was drawing from the mob, asked an old Chicago friend, Frank Cullota, to organize a crack burglary crew and lead it in Vegas. This "Hole-in-the-Wall" gang would commit countless burglaries in the area, with a large percentage going directly to The Ant.

With Outfit leaders back in Chicago already grumbling, Spilotro added icing to the cake by starting an affair with the wife of his supposed partner, "Lefty" Rosenthal. This was a definite mob taboo; wives of associates were considered off-limits.

When Spilotro's Hole-in-the-Wall gang was busted red-handed during a burglary in 1981, things unraveled quickly. When his right-hand man, Cullota, learned that Tony (fearing that Cullota would flip and testify against him) had issued a hit order on him, Cullota decided that he indeed would turn State's witness. Since Spilotro had discarded loyalty, so would Cullota. Frank Cullota, to both save his own life and avoid a long prison sentence, began to sing like a canary to the authorities.

Tony Spilotro was now in it up to his neck, facing an upcoming trial and the wrath of his superiors. But when he was ordered back to Chicago in June of 1986, he went. Ostensibly, the reason was to promote both The Ant and his younger brother, Michael, up the Outfit ladder. Michael, who worshipped Tony and worked hard to emulate him, had basked in the shadow of his brother's glory for some time, although up to now been operating only relatively minor mob enterprises (mostly run from a restaurant he owned on North Avenue).

Tony Spilotro had to have been very suspicious. It was no secret that the Outfit was troubled by the goings-on in Las Vegas. But, a good mob soldier to the heart, he consented to attend the meeting, scheduled for June 14. Still, both Spilotro brothers prepared for the worst. They left their jewelry and other valuables at home (in Oak Park) before leaving for the scheduled meeting. Michael even told his wife, "If we're not back by 9:00, it's no good."[4]

They drove off to a meeting spot and were never seen alive again. Later, their abandoned car was found in a motel parking lot near O'Hare Airport.

On June 23, a farmer in northwestern Indiana came upon an odd sight on the edge of his corn field; it appeared there had been recent digging. At first, believing that a poacher had buried a deer on his property, he notified authorities. An investigation discovered the badly beaten, decomposing bodies of Tony and Michael Spilotro several feet beneath the soil.

In the film *Casino*, the beating deaths of the Spilotros were portrayed as taking place at the cornfield; this was not true.

In the later "Family Secrets" trial in Chicago, Outfit soldier Nick Calabrese claimed the brothers had met a contact near O'Hare, then had been driven to a house in Bensenville, IL. There, they were greeted by fellow mob members and lured to the basement for their "promotion ceremony." A host of wiseguys were waiting. Michael was grabbed and quickly strangled while being pummeled. Tony was made to watch. When it was his turn, The Ant asked his tormenters if he could say a prayer. His request was denied, and he was also beaten to a pulp and strangled.

The rise and fall of The Ant is perhaps the ultimate Outfit cautionary tale.

Spilotro's Boyhood Home. 2152 N. Melvina Avenue, Chicago IL 60639. Spilotro's dad, Pasquale, did not settle in The Patch (the Grand Avenue and Ogden Avenue area, where his restaurant was located. He provided well for his family with the purchase of this more middle-class home in a less volatile area of Chicago.

Note: Home still here.

A Spilotro Home at Time of Death. 1102 S. Maple Avenue, Oak Park IL 60304. The Spilotro brothers left this Oak Park townhome for their doomed 'promotion ceremonies on June 14,

1986. This home is awfully close to the home (and 1974 death site) of Sam Giancana. Coincidence?

Note: I've done a lot of digging into the identification of the house in Bensenville where the Spilotros' met their end, but to no avail. Yet.

Hoagie's Restaurant (owned by Michael Spilotro). Now 6978 Soul Food. 6978 W. North Avenue, Chicago IL 60707.

Note: Michael's restaurant was only about one block from Mad Sam DeStefano's home/death site.

*Patsy's Restaurant: Tony's Dad's Restaurant. 470 N. Ogden Avenue, Chicago IL 60642 (rear of building).*The meatball sandwiches were said to be fabulous.

John Dillinger

Okay, John Dillinger wasn't technically a Chicago Outfit gangster, but he did hang around the city a lot, and he did wind up getting bumped off here. He was, of course, the quintessential charismatic American bank robber, and I'm confident you are pretty familiar with his story. You may have even seen the 2009 film *Public Enemies*, in which Johnny Depp portrayed him (for me, this was about the same as Barry Manilow portraying John Wayne).

I know I've already explained in the Introduction that we are going to skip a visit to the Biograph Theater (where Dillinger met his fate), and instead explore two more off-the-beaten-path sites, but now I'm feeling a little guilty. I guess I should at least list it, just in case you haven't already visited it.

The Biograph Theater. 2433 N. Lincoln Avenue, Chicago IL 60614. On the night of July 22, 1934, FBI agents ambushed Dillinger as he exited the theater. He had watched a Clark Gable film, entitled *Manhattan Melodrama*. He had been set up by madame Anna Sage, a woman he trusted.

Dillinger ran into the alley a few yards away before collapsing from four bullet wounds.

Note: The ghost tour guides will try to convince you the alley is haunted by Dillinger's ghost. Don't fall for it.

Trivia: Dillinger was a big Chicago Cubs fan, attending games at Wrigley Field when in town. If only he could have lived another 84 years …

Dillinger's Plastic Surgery. 2509 N. Pulaski Road (then Crawford) 60639. By early 1934, the heat was really on for John Dillinger. The cops were on the lookout for him—and they knew what he looked like. He decided that a little plastic surgery was just the thing to throw them off the track.

On this site, now a parking lot, stood a house owned by one James "Cabaret" Probasco, a low-level hood and bar owner. Dillinger's crooked attorney, Louis Piquett, arranged for this home to be converted to a makeshift operating theater (for a price, of course), and hired several somewhat shady surgeons to perform the procedure (at a really steep price, of course).

On May 27, Dillinger arrived at the house and prepared for the surgery, scheduled for the following evening. At that time, the doctors arrived and began their work.

It was very nearly a disaster at the start. Mistakes were made with the amount of anaesthesia given to Dillinger and he very nearly died. Luckily for him, things were straightened out and over the course of several evenings, the surgeons did what they could to change his appearance. Plastic surgery in 1934 was still primitive; his face was not really altered as much as he had hoped.

Note: The building is no longer there.

A Dillinger Chicago Hideout. 4310 N. Clarendon, Chicago IL 60613. In the autumn of 1933, Dillinger and his gang rented a six-room apartment on the third floor of this building. According to other tenants (interviewed later), they were "good neighbors," who spent much of their time chatting on the veranda.

Another Dillinger Hideout. 2649 N. Kedzie Ave, Chicago IL 60647. Dillinger once maintained a four-room apartment here (year unknown).

Dillinger's One-Night Hideout Stand. 3512 N. Halsted, Chicago IL 60657. After Dillinger escaped from the Crown Point, Indiana jail, he hightailed it to Chicago in March of 1934, where he spent a night here at the second floor apartment of his girlfriend's sister.

Note: Building still here.

Anna Sage : The Woman in Red Who Betrayed Dillinger. 2858 N. Clark Street, Chicago IL 60657. Anna Sage (real name Ana Cumpanas, dubbed "The Woman in Red" by the press) was a Romanian-born prostitute who ran a brothel on Sheffield Avenue (or Clark Street), but lived in an apartment here. In return for a promise to not be deported, she tipped off the authorities about Dillinger's destination on July 22, 1934: the Biograph Theater. She promised to wear a bright-colored dress that evening to make identification easier.

Note: Sage was actually wearing an orange and white dress on that evening—the bright marquee lights only made it appear red.

Anna Sage's Brothel(s). 3504 N. Sheffield Avenue, Chicago IL 60657 or 3324 N. Clark, Chicago IL 60657. I have gotten conflicting reports on the location of Anna Sage's brothel: Sheffield? Clark? Maybe she was running two of them? At any rate, Sage was conducting her business at the time she agreed to betray John Dillinger from at least one of these locations.

Note: Both buildings remain.

McCready Funeral Home: Where Dillinger was Embalmed.

4506 N. Sheridan Road, Chicago IL 60640. Following his death at the Biograph, Dillinger's body was transported here for embalming. His father would soon arrive to arrange for the transportation of his son's remains to his Indiana hometown.

Over the years, the building, still here, has passed through several hands, serving at one time as a restaurant, a Native American foster care agency, and a homeless shelter for teens. It eventually fell into a state of disrepair before being completely rehabbed in 2017.

Note: The building is still here.

Notable Gangster Sites
The Breeding Ground for the Outfit

There were two main neighborhoods in turn-of-the-century Chicago that were settled by Italian immigrants, and soon became training grounds for young hoods on the rise. In fact, they were thought of as the minor-league teams for the Outfit, learning their larcenous trades there in hopes of one day being promoted to the big leagues. The Outfit big boys would closely monitor the progress of especially promising juvenile thugs.

The neighborhoods were located on the Near West Side of Chicago, and each had their own prominent juvenile gang.

"Little Sicily" aka "Little Hell" (The 42 Gang)
(Roughly) Intersection: Taylor Street and Halsted Street,
Chicago IL 60607
Little Sicily was largely the province of the 42 Gang (so-named because members felt they were just a bit better than Ali Baba's crew). Their main headquarters was Mary's Restaurant at Taylor Street and Loomis Avenue.

Sam Giancana and Mad Sam DeStefano were perhaps the 42 Gang's most famous members.

Mary's Restaurant. (Approx. 1428 W. Taylor Street today).

⌕ *Note:* The area of Little Sicily has been greatly affected by urban renewal, but a leisurely walk from Taylor Street and Halsted westward will still give you a feel of "their turf." Mary's Restaurant is now long gone, but several buildings from the 1920s era remain.

"The Patch" (The Circus Gang)
(Roughly) Intersection: Grand Avenue and Ogden Avenue, Chicago IL 60622

The Circus Gang operated a bit to the northwest of the 42 Gang. The Grand Avenue "corridor," extending both east and west of this intersection was their primary area of predominance. This gang took their name from their headquarters:

The Circus Café at 1857 Grand Avenue, Chicago IL 60622.

The Circus Gang had lots of members soon to become infamous household names in the annals of the Outfit: Tony Accardo, Jack McGurn, "Screwy" Maddox, and "Tough Tony" Capezio.

This area has been completely yuppie-ized, filled with backpack-toting Millennials staring at their phones. The old-time Mustache Petes would hardly recognize it. To attempt to absorb at least a bit of the lingering flavor, spend a little time exploring the intersection of Grand Avenue and Ogden Street. If you are so inclined, a short walk east will take you to the boyhood home of Tony Accardo, Just down the street on Ogden was once the restaurant run by the Spilotro family.

Tony Accardo's Boyhood Home, 1353 W. Grand, Chicago IL 60622.

Gangster Graves
Mount Carmel Cemetery, 1400 S. Wolf Road, Hillside, IL 60162. If you want to see the graves of lots of famous Outfit gangsters, this is the place to go.

Al Capone: Section 35
Dion O'Banion: Section L

Earl "Hymie" Weiss: Section K

Sam Giancana (stone mausoleum): Section 38

Jack "Machine Gun" McGurn (Vincent Gebardi):
   Section O

Vincent ("The Schemer") Drucci (stone mausoleum):
   Section 12

Frank Nitti (Nitto): Section 32

James & Roger Touhy (Towey): Section Q

❀ *Bonus:* An actor who was the absolute best at portraying a real Outfit guy—Dennis Farina: Section 41, Block 21, Lot 6, Grave 1.

Gangster Funeral Homes

Sbarbaro's Funeral Home: Parlor of Choice For Early Mob Royalty,708 N. Wells, Chicago IL 60654. John Sbarbaro was a very interesting guy. Not only did he own a funeral parlor that once stood at this location, he simultaneously served as an assistant district attorney and later, judge. You might say he was working both sides of the fence.

Anyway, several hoods from the Northside O'Banion/Moran gang were laid out in opulent style here: Dion O'Banion, Hymie Weiss, and Vincent "The Schemer" Drucci.

MontClair Lucania Funeral Home: Parlor of Choice For Later Mob Royalty, 6901 W. Belmont Avenue, Chicago IL 60634. In business since 1933, this funeral home served as the last stop for two notable Outfit bigshots, Tony Accardo (1992) and Sam Giancana (1974).

🔍 *Note:* Still here and still doing business.

Salerno's Galewood Chapel: Last Stop for the Spilotro's 1857 N. Harlem Avenue, Chicago, IL 60707. This is where the Spilotro brothers' funeral was held on June 27, 1986. The Roman Catholic Archdiocese of Chicago denied them a traditional mass, but did permit a 15-minute homily service. Outfit leaders were noticeably absent, in mob protocol—a clear sign of disrespect.

This strip of Milwaukee Avenue was once a notorious mob vice haven.

🔎 *Note:* Still here and doing business.

A Sin Strip in an Unlikely Location
  Lone Tree Inn (now the Music Box) 6873 N. Milwaukee Avenue, Niles IL 60714.
  Riviera Lounge (now gone) 6540 N. Milwaukee Avenue, Niles IL 60714.
  Guys & Dolls Tavern (now gone) 6544 N. Milwaukee Avenue, Niles IL 60714.

The area just north of the Milwaukee/Devon intersection is today completely nondescript, but from the 20s all the way into the early 60s, it was something else again. This small pocket of real estate represented the Outfit's vice foray upon Chicago's northwestern city/suburban borderline.

The Capone gang struggled here for control of the beer trade with the much smaller Touhy gang. Big Al himself would occasionally make a personal visit to a roadhouse known as

The Lone Tree Inn during the attempts to reach an agreement with the "Terrible Touhys."

The Touhys refused to give in and remained antagonistic to the Capone gang. One leader, John Touhy, even openly insulted the Capone faction, never a particularly great idea. He would be gunned down inside the Lone Tree in 1927.

Their power soon eroded, but the Outfit never forgot the problems the Touhys had caused. In 1959, another leader, Roger Touhy, was finally released from prison after serving years for a Capone-led frame up involving a kidnap. He was gunned down on his sister's porch. Supposedly, he said, "I've been expecting it. Those bastards never forget."

By the 50s and early 60s, this strip of land still had a few roadhouses/taverns, which in reality, were fronts for the gambling and prostitution rackets. The Riviera Lounge and the Guys and Dolls Tavern, in particular, were constantly raided. In 1959, an exotic dancer was murdered at the Riviera. For good measure,her husband and brother-in-law were also soon whacked.

Today, traveling along Milwaukee Avenue through this completely nondescript strip of land adjacent to tranquil St. Adalbert's Cemetery, it's hard to imagine that it was the scene of such rampant vice activities.

❀ Bonus / While You're Here:

The Grave of Papa Bear George Halas
St. Adalbert's Catholic Cemetery 6800 N. Milwaukee Avenue,
Niles IL 60714. Section 2, Lot 21, Block A
(a small stone mausoleum)

Since you are right at the gates of St. Adalbert's Cemetery, why not pop in to pay your respects to the father of pro football, George "Papa Bear" Halas?

Halas was instrumental in the formation of the league one day to be known as the NFL, starting a pro team dubbed the "Decatur Staleys" in 1920. Those Staleys would soon become better known as the Chicago Bears. Halas was not only the team's owner, he also served several stints as head coach. He was notably cheap, once being described by legendary player/ coach Mike Ditka as a man "who throws around nickels like manhole covers."

Little Known Fact: Halas narrowly avoided becoming a victim in Chicago's tragic Eastland Disaster. In 1915, he was working for the Western Electric Company when employees were invited to board the Eastland passenger ship for a cruise and picnic excursion. He was running late and missed the boarding.

The Eastland, while still moored its Chicago River berth, capsized, drowning 844 people, including many women and children just yards from shore. Sometimes tardiness can really pay off.

Jack Ruby's Grave
Westlawn Cemetery, 7801 W. Montrose Avenue, Norridge IL 60706. Violet Section, Plot 2, Lot 9

Jeez, do I really have to explain who Jack Ruby was? Okay, Millennials: Ruby, born Jacob Rubenstein, was a Chicago-born, mobbed-up burlesque house owner operating out of Dallas, Texas, in 1963. We are supposed to believe that in a

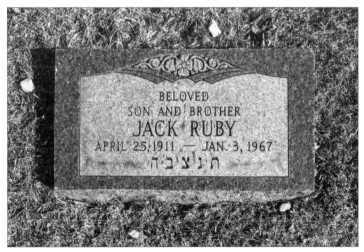

A key figure in the JFK assassination rests at Westlawn Cemetery. Who knew?

moment of patriotic fervor days after the assassination of President John F. Kennedy, he stepped out of a crowd watching Lee Harvey Oswald, the alleged assassin, being transported from the Dallas police station to another facility, and killed him with a handgun.

Uh huh.

Ruby was convicted of murder and remained in prison in Dallas until his death in 1967. He constantly begged members of the Warren Commission (the group charged with investigating the Kennedy assassination) to transfer him to a Washington, DC facility. He promised to reveal the "real truth" about his involvement in the events if only this were done. He constantly claimed that his life was in danger in Dallas, adding "I want to tell the truth, but I can't here."[5]

In October of 1966, Ruby was finally granted a new trial, with a change of venue that would have gotten him out of Dallas, but before this could take place, his health took a mysterious turn for the worse. Admitted to a hospital in December to treat a case of pneumonia, doctors discovered that his body had somehow become quickly riddled with cancer: liver, lungs and brain. Of course. He died just three quick weeks after diagnosis. His body was taken back here to Westlawn Cemetery to be buried beside his parents.

Nothing to see here, folks. Don't ask questions. Just move along.

The Everleigh Club: Chicago's Legendary House of Ill Repute
2133 S. Dearborn Avenue, Chicago IL 60616

The building is long gone, but on this site once stood the elegant Everleigh Club, surely the most luxurious house of prostitution Chicago would ever know. Ada and Minna Everleigh, two enterprising sisters, opened the club in 1900 and spared no expense to impress patrons. Perfumed fountains, costly Persian rugs, gold-rimmed china, mirrored ceilings, library, art gallery and $15,000 gold-leafed piano were only some of the ornate trappings the Everleighs provided for the pleasure of their well-heeled clients. Here, they could relax in style before being escorted upstairs by an "Everleigh Butterfly."

The club drew a lot of heat from city leaders bent on reform. They would eventually get their way; the Everleigh Club was shut down on October 24, 1911. Curiously, Minna and Ada would always claim that top Chicago politicians (you know, those reform-minded ones?) would always receive services free of charge.

Note: That weird "romantic" custom of drinking champagne from a lady's slipper began here in 1902. It was then that a member of Prince Henry of Prussia's staff (the Prince was gracing the club with his exalted presence for a party) drank the bubbly from a prostitute's slipper— and thus began the custom.

Greatest Hits

The Park Ridge Elevator Massacre:
Straight Out Of The Movies.
216. W. Higgins Road, Chicago IL 60068

Remember that scene in the Godfather 1 when burly Corleone Family capo Peter Clemenza, wielding a shotgun, ambushed members of a rival crime family in an elevator? Well, here you go.

On the morning of July 22, 1977, a secretary arriving for work at this two-story office building discovered a horrific sight: the bodies of four very dead men sprawled in a blood-spattered elevator. All had been shot multiple times at close range.

Investigators learned that all four victims had been involved in a decidedly shady business venture selling security system products and burglar alarms. It appeared that the real main thrust of the venture was to sell "distributorships" to the gullible. In other words, the company's business plan was nothing more than a pyramid scheme.

Police speculated on a motive. Since all four victims still possessed cash and jewelry, robbery was ruled out. It was either a revenge killing, perhaps perpetrated by a bilked client, or a Mob hit. The execution-style nature of the evidence (the killer/killers had carefully removed shell casings) favored the latter theory. However, no definitive proof of motive has ever been established.

The crime remains unsolved.

⌀*Note:* The office building is now occupied by a law firm.

The Last Supper of Chuckie English:
A Classic Outfit Hit Horwath's Restaurant
1850 N. Harlem Avenue, Elmwood Park IL 60707

His real name was Charles Carmen Inglesia, but he was known in mob circles as Chuckie English. He grew up on the streets of Chicago with boyhood pal Sam Giancana, and as Giancana rose through the Outfit ranks, he brought Chuckie right along with him. By the 60s, he was functioning as a top lieutenant for Sam, while involved in bookmaking, juice loans, and the vending machine business.

After Giancana was whacked in June of 1975, English's mob clout quickly eroded. New bosses seemed determined to diminish his influence, and with Giancana out of the way, this was steadily accomplished. Stung by his loss of power, English even left Chicago for a few years.

He returned by the early 80s, although now reduced to running only lower level crime action. This was not a good move, although exactly why is unclear.

On February 13, 1985, (Valentine's Day eve—what is it about the Outfit and Valentine's Day?) Chuckie visited this restaurant for a meal. As he later left and headed for the parking lot, two men in ski masks strolled up and riddled him with bullets—one right between the eyes. The murder remains unsolved.

Alas, Horwath's is yet another victim of changing times. An office supply store first occupied the original site. Two new businesses have now replaced it.

Note: As a teenager, I had dinner at Horwath's a couple of times. It never occurred to me then that the place was mobbed-up. Who thinks of stuff like that when they're in their teens? It did have a very distinctive old-school vibe to it—lots of older, pinky ring-type fellows with thin, pale women.

Horwath's always provided a complimentary relish tray with every dinner.

Which was nice.

The Allen Dorfman Hit: The Man Who Knew Too Much
Lincolnwood Hyatt Hotel
(Later known as "The Purple Hotel")
4500 Touhy Avenue, Lincolnwood IL 60712

The best place to start here is with another movie reference. Do you remember the scene in Martin Scorcese's film *Casino* where the mobbed-up businessman character (portrayed by actor/comedian Alan King) gets whacked in a parking lot? Well, that character was based on Allen Dorfman.

Dorfman was the Outfit's money man—and he knew a lot. In fact, he knew where virtually all of their financial bodies were buried. And his vast, firsthand knowledge of the mob's illegal manipulations of union pension funds and Las Vegas casino skimming had made him a most attractive target for the Feds. As a bonus, since he had been very close to Teamsters one-time leader, Jimmy Hoffa, it was rumored that he could even answer a few questions about his mysterious disappearance back in 1975.

In January of 1983, Dorfman was facing a long prison term after being convicted of the bribery of a US senator in a shady real estate scheme in Nevada. And the Outfit was very nervous. If Dorfman, then almost 60, blanched at the prospect of what could well be a life sentence and decided to talk to save his skin, a lot of Outfit higher-ups would be keeping him company in the slammer. What to do?

If Dorfman had been a Sicilian and embraced the tradition of omerta, things might have been different. But he was not a Sicilian. So the Outfit, as it usually did, chose the route of caution. After all, why take a chance?

On a cold Thursday afternoon on January 20, 1983, Dorfman and a business associate walked through the icy parking lot here on their way to the hotel coffee shop. Two men wearing ski masks suddenly appeared from behind and one of them put six, .22 caliber bullets into Dorfman's head.

Problem resolved.

The Strange Case of the Candy Lady: The Helen Brach Mystery
830 Eastwood Lane, Glenview IL 60025

The Helen Brach case is not your typical mob hit, but it most definitely was a hit. And it didn't even involve the Outfit. The group responsible was every bit as ruthless, and maybe even less principled: the shadowy Chicago-area horse ring. This group was led by a particularly nasty bit of business named Silas Jayne. Jayne had served time for rape, and would be later linked to all sorts of nefarious activities, including blackmail and even the murder of his half-brother. (See the Peterson-Schuessler Murders).

Although Jayne was a successful man, and owned many horses and stables in the Chicago area, he found that supplying riding lessons and pony rides were not bringing in the kind of income he wanted. The real money, he found, could be made in selling horses; to be precise, the selling of worthless horses to gullible wealthy people for vast sums.

Heiress Helen Voorhees Brach must have seemed like the ideal mark: newly widowed, attractive, lonely, and very, very rich. The icing on the cake: she was a devout animal lover. With the death of her candy company tycoon husband in 1970, Helen came to the attention of the Jayne gang. She seemed to be extremely ripe for the plucking.

Richard Bailey, a close associate of Silas Jayne, was chosen for the task. The main attribute in Bailey's toolbox was smooth charm. He had a long history of first befriending and then defrauding wealthy widows with sales of worthless horses. Bailey immediately began working his magic with the 65-year-old Helen. Soon they were wining, dining and dancing the nights away in the city or relaxing together in her stately Glenview home.

And soon, Helen was purchasing horses—for lots of money- on Bailey's equine recommendations. The horses would be later appraised by experts as virtually worthless.

Glen Grove Equestrian Center. 9453 Harms Road, Morton Grove IL 60053. Richard Bailey owned this stable while courting Helen Brach.

Helen Brach eventually realized that she had been swindled and began telling acquaintances that she was going to do something about it. Word of this had to get back quickly to the Jayne gang.

On February 17, 1977, Brach left the Mayo Clinic in Minneapolis after her yearly checkup. She was scheduled to fly back to Chicago that day. A gift shop assistant would later claim that she overheard Brach say, "I'm in a hurry, my houseman is waiting."

That was the last time Helen Brach was ever officially seen. The airline claimed she never boarded the return flight to O'Hare, but she might have, perhaps deciding to travel by car. But for all intents and purposes, she simply vanished. However, there are some who insist she did make it home to her Glenview estate.

Things then got really murky. Helen's houseman was an ex-con named Jack Matlick. He would claim he had no knowledge of anything. A particularly juicy aspect of all this is that Matlick had recently purchased an industrial-grade meat grinder for the Brach home. Oh, and Helen had five dogs. Five dogs with healthy appetites.

With no body, investigators found that identifying the murderers pretty much impossible. Richard Bailey would eventually be charged and convicted in connection to the case—not for murder, just "conspiracy." He received a 30-year sentence.

Silas Jayne was also convicted on a conspiracy charge— but not one connected to the Brach case. Jayne was found guilty of involvement in his step-brother's murder. After serving his sentence, he was released and died of leukemia in 1987.

Ex-con Matlick was never charged with a crime.

So—what happened to Helen Brach? The most plausible

answer probably comes from the unsubstantiated claims and tips offered at various times by fringe crime figures, in many cases attempting to barter "inside knowledge" for lighter treatment. The common theme shared with these tips: that Helen Brach was silenced by the horse–swindling gang before she could do them any real damage. She was beaten to death, it was said, then her body taken across the Indiana border to a steel mill, where it was incinerated.

Note: The Brach house is only about one and a half miles from my home. Whenever I drive past it with a friend unfamiliar with the story, I relate it as a point of interest. (My wife worries about my social skills a lot.) For some reason, the part they invariably like best is the one about the meat grinder purchase.

The Fox Lake Massacre
Manning Hotel (then) 14 N. Pistakee Road, Fox Lake IL 60020
Sleepy Fox Lake is part of the Chain o' Lakes recreational area, today a haven for the Jimmy Buffet boating crowd. You surely must be familiar with them: the mostly middle-aged, hippie-types who love to dock their modest boats at waterfront bars, call each other "man" (ad nauseum), and spend days and night getting totally wasted in their Midwest version of Margaritaville.

But in 1930, the area was being hotly contested by gangsters; at stake was control of the liquor trade. And it was here, at an indoor porch area of what was then the Manning Hotel, that four mob-connected characters, plus a woman drinking with them, were machinegunned in a sneak attack.

The exact reasons for the attack are pretty murky. The owner of the hotel had recently changed beer distributors, which of course did not please the previous one. Since the victims had ties to the Capone gang, there are some who claim the hit was revenge for the St. Valentine's Day Massacre. There is also some evidence that a freelance hitman named Vernon Miller masterminded the attack in retaliation for the Capone gang's whacking of a friend.

Here's what is known: At 1:40 AM on June 1, 1930, a group sat drinking in the enclosed porch area of the hotel, facing the lake. Gunmen crept up in the darkness and opened up with Thompson submachine guns.

Killed were Mike Quirk (Klondike O'Donnell gang—Capone allies), Sam Pellar (Capone gang), Joe Bertsche (Drugaan-Lake gang—also Capone allies).

Wounded were George Druggan, brother of the head of the Druggan-Lake gang, and Vivian McGinnis, girlfriend of George. The crime remains unsolved to this day.

🔎 *Note:* The building, now a private residence, is still there, next to a funeral parlor. To view the crime site, you need to get to the rear parking area of the funeral parlor and look to the north side, near the lake.

The Citizen Cain Hit: Whose side was he on?
1117 W. Grand Avenue Chicago IL 60642
(then Rose's Sandwich Shop)

Richard Cain was a most interesting and shadowy character in the traditionally corrupt marriage of Chicago politics and the Outfit. His kaleidoscopic career was almost beyond belief. At various times, he was allegedly a member of the city police force (it was rumored that he had been "planted" there by the Mob as a spy), a chief investigator for the Cook County Sheriff's office, a liaison between the Outfit and corrupt police officials, a convict convicted of perjury, of being an accessory to a bank robbery, a close advisor to Outfit boss Sam Giancana (he served as Giancana's right hand man in gambling operations run from Mexico), and toward the end of his life, an FBI informant.

Oh, and by the way—he was rumored to be involved in the ill-fated U.S. Bay of Pigs invasion—and the Kennedy assassination.

In short, Richard Cain took "working both sides of the street" to a whole new level. Upon release from his prison stint in 1971, things, however, looked decidedly bleaker for him. Not only were his police connections long gone, his old friend

Giancana had seemed to have turned his back on him. It was at this time that Cain allegedly offered his services to the FBI as an informer on mob activities. Word soon got back to Outfit leaders, who were definitely not pleased. Word came down from the higher-ups to take him out.

On December 20, 1973, Cain was meeting with four men at this location, then Rose's Sandwich Shop. Shortly after the men left, two masked gunmen, carrying walkie-talkies, entered the shop. After lining the patrons up, they separated Cain from the rest. According to later witness testimonies, the gunmen then received an "all clear" message on the walkie-talkies. A blast from a sawed-off shotgun immediately took off half of Cain's face; a coup de grace pistol shot to his head made sure.

The neighborhood, once the very heart of the Little Italy area of Chicago (and the minor league training ground for young hoods) has undergone considerable gentrification over the years. Rose's Sandwich Shop is no more. The storefront has had several new incarnations since 1973.

The Family Secrets Hit: Bingo!
6050 W. Belmont Avenue, Chicago IL 60634
This poorly-carried-out hit by the Outfit on one of its own members would play a large role in the takedown of many high-ranking Chicago mobsters in what became known as "The Family Secret"' affair.

In 1986, longtime mob associate John Fecarotta had come into disfavor with higher-ups, and word came down that he was to be eliminated. The job was assigned to the particularly vicious street crew led by Frank Calabrese, an enforcer feared throughout Chicago. Frank, in turn, delegated the task to his young brother, Nick, a somewhat more reluctant—and far less violent—member of the crew. In the Outfit, however, orders were orders. Nick Calabrese would later testify that he had little doubt that if he refused the mission, his own life would be forfeited.

On September 14, 1986, Nick Calabrese, accompanied by Fecarotta, pulled into an alley just south of Belmont Avenue.

The cover story created to lure an unsuspecting Fecarotta into the trap was that a local dentist had crossed the Outfit, and his office was to be bombed. Calabrese needed an accomplice to help out, and Fecarotta was simply the designated choice.

Fecarotta, though, apparently had his gangster antenna up; when Calabrese suddenly went for a handgun, a struggle broke out. The gun went off, striking Calabrese in the arm. Fecarotta was out of the car in a flash and running for his life, his attacker in hot pursuit. Crossing Belmont, he made it to the entrance of a bingo parlor on the north side of the street. That's as far as he got. Nick Calabrese, despite bleeding from his arm wound, caught up with him there and shot him in the head.

Before Calabrese could locate the getaway car (the botched nature of the hit had affected logistics), he made a crucial error: unknowingly, he dropped the gloves he had been wearing while carrying out the shooting. These would soon be found by the police.

The dropped gloves containing Calabrese's DNA plus the bullet fragments in his arm, found later during a police-ordered X-ray, would enable police to firmly pin a murder rap on him, and ultimately get him to "turn"—to become the first made man to agree to testify against his comrades in the Chicago Outfit, including his own brother.

The trial would prove to be a blockbuster. All Chicago was riveted on the proceedings: would the canary sing? And sing he did. Nick Calabrese spilled his guts on countless mob crimes dating back decades. Many top-ranking members of the Outfit would be convicted of various nefarious activities and sent away for long prison stretches. In many ways, this affair was a backbreaker for the Chicago Outfit. Nick Calabrese, himself, would receive a greatly reduced sentence for his cooperation and eventually be released (in 2012) into the Witness Protection Program. As of September, 2019, he was still free—and un-whacked.

The building where the "hit heard round the world" took place is still here, though it seems to be a church now.

✐ *Note:* My mom used to play bingo at this Belmont Avenue (former) bingo parlor.

Andrew Cunanan: A Psychopath's Deadly Visit to Chicago
24 E. Scott Street, Chicago IL 60610

Andrew Cunanan was a gay, young hustler forever orbiting the circles of rich and powerful men, seeking entry into a world of wealth and privilege. Operating primarily out of San Diego, San Francisco and Scottsdale, Cunanan offered his services to affluent men who would support him and provide the lavish lifestyle he felt he deserved.

By 1997, due to an overwhelming frustration with his inability to form the lasting relationship he so desperately desired, Cunanan hit a breaking point. He embarked on a cross-county journey leaving five men dead, including at least three he deemed had abandoned/crossed him.

Cunanan's murder spree would eventually end with the notorious murder of designer Gianni Versace in front of his Miami Beach mansion on July 15 and Cunanan's subsequent suicide while hiding out on a houseboat in the area.

But prior to that, Andrew Cunanan, having already committed two murders of now-estranged former friends in the Minneapolis area, headed for Chicago. The reason is unclear. Arriving on May 4, he would quickly claim his third victim, prominent real estate tycoon Lee Miglin. There is absolutely no hard evidence connecting him to Cunanan. Miglin's family has always vehemently denied any link between the two men. The millionaire's death may simply have been a case of being in the wrong place at the wrong time. He may simply have been a random Gold Coast target for Cunanan's flourishing homicidal rage.

Whatever the motive and circumstances, Cunanan brutally murdered Lee Miglin. When police entered his stately home on E. Scott, they discovered a scene of extreme carnage. Miglin's body was found in the garage. His hands and feet had been bound; his face and head completely wrapped in tape plastic and paper, leaving only a small opening for breathing.

The killer had clearly taken his time murdering the unfortunate man. Miglin's ribs were broken, his chest punctured repeatedly with garden shears, and his throat torn open by a saw-like instrument. In addition, conditions in the house confirmed that Cunanan had been in no hurry. He had apparently slept in Miglin's bed, consumed a ham sandwich, helped himself to a large amount of cash, and had a bath and shave in the bathroom before departing. The fact that there were no signs of forced entry into the home puzzled police, and forced them to at least question the notion that the murder was a completely random occurrence.

Cunanan would next continue his murderous rampage in New Jersey, where he killed a cemetery caretaker to gain possession of his truck before heading south to Florida for his deadly July encounter with Gianni Versace.

✐ *Notes:*

1. Lee Miglin's wife was Home Shopping Network's queen Marilyn Miglin, who was out of town at the time of the murder. She continues to this day to deny that Lee knew Cunanan.

2. In high school, Andrew Cunanan was voted by his classmates "least likely to be forgotten."

Baby Face Nelson's Last Ride
227 W. Northwest Highway, Barrington IL 60010
(the "Barrington Shootout")
1627 Walnut Street, Wilmette IL 60091 (where Nelson died)
St. Paul's Lutheran Cemetery, Harms Road, Niles IL 60077
(where his body was found)

Baby Face Nelson (real name Lester Joseph Gillis) was born in Chicago in 1908. He entered a life of crime at an early age, delivering bootleg booze while still in his teens. He soon joined a suburban gang and became involved in armed robberies.

By 1930, he was robbing banks and committing home invasions. The home of Chicago mayor Big Bill Thompson was even robbed; the mayor's wife described the thief thusly: "He had a baby face. He was good-looking, hardly more than a boy…"[6] The nickname stuck.

Nelson and company employed ever-increasing violent tactics with each passing crime: a botched roadhouse robbery resulted in the deaths of three men, and a subsequent tavern stick-up ended with the death of a prominent stockbroker.

Nelson was arrested in late 1931 but managed to escape in February of the following year. He fled west and continued his criminal exploits in California for a short period. Forming his own gang, he returned to the Midwest, where he even allied with the legendary John Dillinger for a time before Dillinger was gunned down in July of 1934.

Nelson was soon declared Public Enemy Number One by J. Edgar Hoover as the bank robberies continued. He was all of 25 years old.

On November 27, 1934, Baby Face, his wife, Helen, and a gang accomplice named John Paul Chase were headed south to Chicago from a hideout in Lake Geneva, along Highway 14. Along the way, they attracted the attention of federal agents. A car chase ensued. Nelson's car came to a stop at a park in Barrington and a furious gun battle erupted, near the spot where the McDonald's is today.

Nelson, ever fearless (and reckless) charged the agents with a machine gun, receiving nine bullet wounds- but managing to injure his opponents. The firing stopped and Nelson was lifted into the outlaw car by Helen and Chase. They sped off, headed south.

The gang finally reached the home of a friend in Wilmette. Nelson was carried in and a doomed attempt was made to address his wounds. At last he gasped out his last words: "It's getting dark, Helen. I can't see you anymore," and died.

Helen and Chase wrapped him in a blanket and, unsure what to do, decided to leave his body in a place where it would be almost immediately found. They drove southwest to Niles, found a small cemetery, and deposited the body on the grassy area outside the fence, near the southwest corner of Conrad Street and Long Avenue. An anonymous call to a funeral parlor, and a subsequent call to the police, led to the

The body of Baby Face Nelson was found here in Skokie.

quick discovery of Nelson. He was transported to the Cook County morgue, where an estimated 2,000 curious people had the chance to file past his body.

Note: St. Paul's Lutheran Cemetery, of course, has not changed much since 1934, so it's easy to imagine Nelson's "dump spot" outside the fence.

Baby Face Nelson Grave (Lester Gillis): St. Joseph Cemetery. Belmont & Cumberland Avenues, River Grove IL 60171 Section C, Lot 18, Block 8. You really didn't expect his gravestone to read "Baby Face," did you?

3. MONSTERS OF THE MIDWAY

H. H. Holmes: The Devil in Chicago

With the success of author Erik Larson's "Devil in the White City," many, many people are now familiar with the name H. H. Holmes and have at least a general notion of his crimes.

Still, it might be helpful to lay out some basics.

It should be mentioned at the outset that Holmes' image in popular culture shares a striking similarity with that of another legendary Chicago boogeymen, Al Capone. The nefarious exploits of both men were prodigiously inflated, both during their lifetimes and after. The popular press was the main instigator, but Holmes himself did little to clarify matters, by constantly claiming responsibility (and often later retracting the claims) for many more deaths than can be attributed to him.

Top 10 H. H. Holmes in a Nutshell:

1. H. H. Holmes (real name Herman Mudgett) was a University of Michigan-trained doctor. He arrived in Chicago in 1886, age 25.

2. His fellow students (talk about foreshadowing!) would claim that Holmes "delighted in the joys of the dissection room."

3. Although possessing a medical degree (thereby ensur-

ing a good living), Holmes found his true calling as a swindler, huckster and killer.

4.   Holmes was highly unusual among the pantheon of serial killers in two major respects:

a. He was kind of an equal-opportunity murderer. In addition to both men and women, he took the lives of at least three children.

b. He was a true capitalist. All of his known murders involved profit. He would swindle and then murder people. He would also kill to claim insurance money. It's even claimed he would reduce some victims to skeletons and sell the remains to medical schools. Talk about maximizing profits!

5.   Once in Chicago, Holmes quickly began working scams all over town. By 1897, he was building a "hotel" at 63rd and Wallace meant to attract visitors to the upcoming 1893 Columbian Exposition.

6.   Holmes lured many visitors to his "hotel." Unbeknownst to them, the place was designed with murder in mind. Much of the building was riddled with soundproof rooms, secret passages and a disorienting maze of hallways. A trapdoor connected to a chute leading to the basement, which contained a large furnace, quicklime and acid pits. Many visitors to the fair never returned home.

7.   Holmes was finally arrested in Boston in 1984 on charges of killing an associate for insurance money.

8.   Upon his arrest, police acted on the many dark rumors surrounding Holmes and explored his hotel, which was now being called his "murder castle." Despite the unsettling features of the building, little actual hard evidence of foul play was discovered.

9.   Holmes was executed by hanging on May 7, 1896. He previously requested, apparently fearing vengeful graverobbers, that his coffin be encased by an enormous amount of concrete.

10. For many years, the rumor persisted that Holmes the conman had cheated the hangman with well-placed bribes, but a 2017 exhumation put that notion finally to rest. The body in the grave was indeed that of Holmes.

H. H. Holmes's mysterious "glass-blowing" factory (and huge furnace) once stood here.

As I mentioned in the Introduction: I am not going to suggest a trip out to 63rd & Wallace to visit the site of the Holmes notorious "murder castle." It's gone anyway, replaced by a dingy post office. If you really want to go, I'd advise you to sign on to one of the many bus Ghost Tours available in Chicago. That way, you—and thirty others—can be navigated safely through a now decidedly sketchy neighborhood in the comfort of a fortress on wheels. To see a dingy post office.

Now on the other hand, how about a few visits to alternative Holmes-connected sites—ones to which the tour buses don't go? (See how I worked in the title of the book here?)

Let's start with "The (Maybe) Dump Site:"

"Glass-Blowing Factory"/ Dump Site?
(Approx.) 2343 N. Seeley Avenue Chicago IL 60647
("Sobieski Street" in Holmes's time)

As previously noted, the police investigation of Holmes' Murder Castle did not turn up much in the way of solid homicide evidence. Basically, the closest thing were a few bone fragments that may not even have been human (no DNA testing in 1885).

So then, we know that Holmes killed people, but where did he dispose of the remains?

Well, there is a small area in Chicago that might hold the key.

H. H. Holmes appeared to be fascinated with glass-blowing. Now the glass-blowing process requires a large, very efficient furnace. Holmes had a very large and efficient furnace–150 feet long!—constructed here. There was a small house here, too.

Since no actual glass products ever seemed to be produced, the question might be asked: "Why might a known serial killer be interested in a huge furnace?" Hmm …

It is known that several women involved with Holmes lived in the immediate neighborhood, and that they disappeared without a trace.

This pocket-sized area, until recently, was pretty much a secluded little wasteland. Now, of course, it's gentrified with those inevitable condos.

🔍 *Note:* The address listed is approximate. The furnace and house were just about here.

The Candy Man Can: Holmes's Candy Store
1513 N. Milwaukee Avenue, Chicago IL 60622

This was the site of a candy store owned by Holmes under an assumed name (Frank Wilde). Why the assumed name? Don't know, but it had to involve some kind of scam.

A young woman, one Emily Van Tassel, worked at this store, and lived nearby. Holmes had some sort of romantic attachment with her. After her disappearance, her mother would claim they had been on several dates.

She has never been positively labeled a Holmes murder victim, but likely was. No body? No problem. Please note that the candy store address is only 1.2 miles away from the glass-blowing factory location.

🔍 *Note:* The store is gone now, replaced by a modern storefront.

Wilmette Home
726 11th Street, Wilmette IL 60091
(originally 38 N. St. John Street)

Holmes "lived" here at least in theory but seemed to spend little time at the residence. Most of the time, it seemed to be just wife Myrta, daughter Lucy, and Myrta's parents. He commuted to Chicago constantly, often spending long periods of time there, perpetrating countless scams, and constructing his infamous "hotel" in Englewood before returning to Wilmette. Upon his arrest in 1895, reporters besieged this place, hounding Myrta Holmes mercilessly for interviews. She claimed that she could believe Holmes was guilty of swindling, but did not believe him capable of murder.

🔍 *Note:* The home was torn down in 1997 and replaced by townhomes and condos. Naturally. Why, oh why, do so many interesting sites get replaced by townhomes and condos?

Holmes's Rented Apartment
1140 W. Wrightwood, Chicago IL 60614

In 1893, Holmes rented the top floor apartment for his fiancée, Mississippi-born Minnie Williams. He was desperate to keep her away from his nefarious activities at his "Murder Castle" on the South Side. Holmes was no doubt interested in Minnie's considerable inheritance money. She knew him as "Henry Gordon." He convinced her that he only used "H. H. Holmes" for business dealings in Chicago.

Minnie was soon joined by a sister, Anna. The two sisters were known to have made several visits to the World's Fair on the lake front. On July 5, 1893, Holmes invited Anna for a personally-escorted tour of his "hotel" at 63rd and Wallace. Later the same day, he sent for Minnie to join them. Both women were never seen alive again.

John Wayne Gacy:
Chicago's Very Own Killer Clown

The subject of John Wayne Gacy and his horrific Chicago-area murders of young men has been done to death, so to speak. There are books and videos galore out there dealing with all the gory details. Since you have decided to read this book, I think I can safely assume that you are already more than a bit familiar with the name and have at least a general knowledge of the crimes.

Still, I feel compelled to offer at least this, just in case:

1.   Gacy was an outwardly normal and gregarious Chicago-area contractor.

2.   He worked hard to "hide in plain sight" as a pillar of his community, joining civic groups, doing political work, and even entertaining children as "Pogo the Clown."

3.   He was a prolific and voracious serial killer. He murdered at least 33 young men.

4.   Gacy's M.O.: entice vulnerable young men to his suburban home with promises of money, a job, or lodging, subdue them with a "handcuff trick," abuse them, then murder them.

5.   Many of his victims (29) were buried in the crawlspace and backyard of his home.

6.   His killing spree lasted from (approx.) 1972–1978, ending with his arrest on December 21, 1978.

7.   Gacy was described thusly by his attorney: "And that was the scariest thing about him, contrary to how he was portrayed in television and movies. He was a little Santa Claus jolly looking kind of guy."

8.   He was put to death by lethal injection on May 10, 1994. His last words? "Kiss my ass."

John Wayne Gacy's Boyhood Home
4505 N. Marmora Avenue, Chicago, IL 60630

The Gacy family moved into this bungalow in 1952, when John Wayne was about ten. Here, he spent his very unhappy teen tears, tormented by an abusive, alcoholic father.

John Wayne Gacy's Home (where the bodies were buried)
Summerdale Avenue, Chicago IL 60656

I am not going to supply an exact address—the folks living here now don't need any more grief. In fact, in an attempt to keep the curious away after the events, the addresses were shuffled.

Still, if you are really hardcore about it, you could simply stroll around the 8200 Summerdale block west of N. Pioneer Avenue. For heaven's sake, try not to look too obvious. You might possibly find a house that looks a little out of place on the southern side of the street, maybe just a little too new to fit in with the others.

Buried beneath the soil of this property were the bodies of 29 young victims.

Onward!

Bonus: OJ Simpson in Chicago

Holiday Inn Chicago O'Hare (where OJ got that call)
5615 N. Cumberland Avenue, Chicago IL 60631
(only ½ mile north)

As long as you are headed north, to reach your next Gacy site, you might consider a quick stop at the hotel where OJ was staying in June 1994 (only a month after John Wayne Gacy left this mortal coil), when he received the call from the LA police informing him of his wife's murder. Boy, can you imagine his surprise?

It's now a Holiday Inn, but back then it was the O'Hare Plaza Hotel. Simpson's room was 915. The police, once they began to smell something fishy, searched this room to find a bloody towel and a broken glass. (Simpson claimed the cuts on his hand were caused by this broken glass. After all, he was distraught. Of course.)

On a side note, and I know it's going to sound like a load of nonsense (but it's absolutely true). I believe I smelled something fishy at least as early as the police did—and carried out my own unofficial investigation before they did.

At the time, like most crime aficionados, I fancied myself a bit of a junior detective. When the news about the events broke and details were trickling in (murder by person—or persons—unknown), I got the bright idea that Simpson himself was guilty. Since no murder weapon/knife had been found at the Brentwood killing scene, where was it? *Eureka!* I thought. OJ must have transported the evidence linking him to the crime far away—Chicago! How? His golf bag, of course!

I drove out to the hotel and spent a few hapless hours searching the parking area and an adjacent field to the south.

I'm a lousy detective.

Now it's on to another Gacy site.

Back to John Wayne Gacy

The Pharmacy (where Gacy met his last victim)
1920 E. Touhy Avenue, Des Plaines IL 60018
Now a daycare center, in December of 1978 it was the Nissan Pharmacy. Fifteen-year-old Robert Piest was working a part-time shift there on the night of the 11th when he was approached by a burly man who identified himself as a local contractor seeking young men for high-paying work. The man was John Wayne Gacy.

Piest went off into the night with him and was never seen alive again. His body would be found floating in the nearby Des Plaines River the following April.

A film receipt that was linked to Piest, later found by investigators in Gacy's home, would prove to be a key piece of evidence in his coming trial and conviction.

Gacy's Lawyer's Office
(where he began a rambling confession)
222 S. Prospect Avenue, Park Ridge IL 60068

Gacy, with the police closing in, visited his lawyer here, downed a few shots of Canadian whiskey, and began a rambling confession lasting hours. Later, his stunned attorney would remark: "It was the longest night of my life." [7]

🔎 *Note:* No longer a law firm, the office is now occupied by the American Association of Nurse Anesthetists.

"Bughouse Square"/Washington Square Park
(a Gacy "hunting area")
901 N. Clark Street, Chicago IL 60610

This small park gained its quaint nickname from older days, when it was a bastion of free speech. Any and all (no matter how buggy) were free to proselytize (probably perched upon soapboxes) on any subject.

Later, the square became kind of a marketplace for young male hustlers.

Gacy often cruised the area for victims.

🔎 *Note:* The park is still here, although no one seems to be making speeches anymore.

The Greyhound Bus Station (another Gacy "hunting area")
161 N. Clark Street, Chicago IL 60601

The bus station is now gone; replaced by a high-rise building. Gacy often cruised this location in search of cash-strapped, vulnerable young men new to the city.

He would later claim to have picked up his very first victim here.

Gacy's Arrest: McDonald's
7969 N. Milwaukee Avenue, Niles IL 60714

On December 21, five policemen pulled over John Wayne Gacy's car in front of this McDonald's and placed him under arrest. I've always found it kind of fitting that "Pogo the Clown" was busted by Ronald McDonald.

In case you are wondering:

If Gacy buried 29 victims in the crawlspace of his home –
what became of the other four? He would later claim that once
his crawlspace became too crowded he began tossing bodies
into the Des Plaines River from the Interstate 55 Bridge southwest of Joliet.

No reason to go; it's a pretty long drive just to see a bridge.

Bonus: Jeffrey Dahmer in Chicago

Carol's Speakeasy, 1355 N. Wells, Chicago IL 60610
Okay, Jeffrey Dahmer was a Milwaukee serial killer/ can-
nibal—but—we know he picked up at least one victim here in
this Chicago gay bar. Jeremiah Weinberger, 23, met Dahmer
here in July of 1991, and accompanied him back to Milwaukee.
His head would later wind up in Dahmer's freezer.

The L&L Tavern on North Clark. John Wayne Gacy and Jeffrey Dahmer
often visited.

🔍 *Note:* Carol's Speakeasy was demolished in 2017.

L&L Tavern (John Wayne Gacy and Jeffrey Dahmer)
3207 N. Clark Street, Chicago IL 60657
This is the only known location where evidence suggests that both John Wayne Gacy and serial killer/cannibal Jeffrey Dahmer scouted for possible victims. Maybe not the best choice for a first date, all things considered.

🔍 *Note:* Still here and in business.

Richard Speck: Born to Raise Hell

If you conducted an internet search under the heading "scummy loser," there's a very good chance a photo of Richard Speck would appear on your screen.

Speck was born in 1941 in Kirkwood, Illinois, a small town just over 200 miles southwest of Chicago. The family soon moved to nearby Monmouth, where his father, whom the six-year-old Speck idolized, died unexpectedly from a heart attack. In 1950 his mother remarried to a man quite different from his father. His new stepfather was a violent, hard-drinking lout who often physically and verbally abused him.

The family relocated to Dallas, where Speck immediately began getting in trouble. Arrests for check fraud and theft, as well as a few more violent episodes, earned him a stint in prison. Paroled after 16 months, he returned to Monmouth, where he raped a 65-year-old woman and was suspected of killing a 32-year-old barmaid.

In 1966, Speck skipped town to avoid questioning and headed to Chicago, where an older sister lived. While staying with her, he attempted to get a seaman's job, applying at the National Maritime Union, located on the city's south side. He soon (April) found a position as a hand on a lake freighter, but was stricken with appendicitis and had to be helicoptered to a nearby hospital for emergency surgery.

By May 20, he had recovered sufficiently to rejoin his shipmates on the freighter, but a drunken quarrel with a ship's officer resulted in his being put ashore on June 20.

By early July, Speck had worn out his welcome at his sister's home and was lodging at cheap motels near the Union as he attempted to once again find work. On July 13, he found that the job he thought he had secured had been given to someone else. Angry and frustrated, he set off on a drug and alcohol-fueled binge that would eventually evolve into a legendary murderous rampage.

He began the night by picking up a 53-year-old woman he had met at a local tavern, bringing her back to his room, raping her and stealing a .22 caliber pistol she carried. He then continued his drinking spree at the bar attached to The Shipyard Inn hotel.

Sometime after 10 PM, Speck, high as a kite and still filled with a murderous rage, set off walking west on 100th street. After traveling one and a half miles, he came upon a townhome that served as residence for nine student nurses working at the South Side Community Hospital.

Armed with a switchblade and the stolen handgun, he gained entry into the home through a window and quickly rounded up the nine women. Using bedsheets, he tied them up, all the while assuring them he meant them no harm; it was merely a robbery. He then began leading the girls, one by one, into another part of the house, where he stabbed and strangled each.

Speck must have lost count of his victims. Unbeknownst to him one, 23-year-old Corazon Amurao, managed to hide beneath a bed while he was in another part of the house. Long after he had finished the carnage and run off into the night, the terrified Amurao remained hidden, only coming out when daylight arrived about 6 AM. She ran to a window and screamed for help.

The police soon arrived at the horrific scene and conducted an investigation. Fingerprints found identified the killer as one Richard Speck and Amurao was able to provide a description. Particularly helpful was the prominent tattoo she said her tormenter had on an arm. The tattoo: "Born to Raise Hell."[8]

Two days later on July 17, a drifter staying at the Starr Hotel, a flophouse on Chicago's skid row, recognized a fellow lodger as Richard Speck and phoned the police. For some reason, the cops failed to respond. Later that night Speck attempted suicide by slitting his wrists and was rushed to the hospital. There, a resident physician noticed the "Born to Raise Hell" tattoo on the patient's arm (which had been widely reported in the newspapers) and notified authorities. This time they did respond and placed Speck under arrest.

Richard Speck was tried and convicted of murder. On April 15, 1967, he was sentenced to death in the electric chair. While on Death Row (1972), Illinois abolished the death penalty; Speck was resentenced to a term of 400-1,200 years. He died from a massive heart attack in prison on the eve of his 50th birthday, December 5, 1991.

Note: Prison certainly seemed to agree with Richard Speck. Videotapes made at Stateville Correctional Center, in Crest Hill, IL were discovered in 1996 and reveal disturbing insights into Speck's life behind bars. He had used smuggled hormone drugs to transition his body. He now resembled a woman far more than a man. He was seen freely exchanging drugs and money with fellow prisoners, openly engaging in sexual activities, and laughing about having almost complete freedom to do whatever he wanted with no fear of punishment. Most chilling: when asked by a fellow inmate if he had indeed committed the notorious student nurse murders, he replied, "Sure I did." When asked why, he shrugged his shoulders and responded, "It just wasn't their night." [9]

Murder Site: The Student Nurses' Townhome
2319 E. 100th Street, Chicago IL 60617

Note: The home still stands.

Speck's Sister's Home
3966 N. Avondale, Chicago IL 60641

Speck stayed here with sister Martha and her family for a few weeks.

The Starr Hotel: Where Richard Speck Attempted Suicide
617 W. Madison Street, Chicago IL 60661

Skid Row is now long gone. The area is known as "The West Loop" and has been completely gentrified. The site where this flophouse once stood is now a huge parking garage for the swanky Presidential Towers apartment complex.

William Heirens: Fiend or Innocent Man?

William Heiren's name appears on this Murderer's Row list of Chicago killers because of the notoriety surrounding his case and the crimes he was accused of. But, there's a possibility that he was an innocent man. To this very day, Heiren's claim that he was tortured into confessions for three heinous crimes receives a lot of support from various sources.

Born in Evanston in 1928, Heirens was raised in an impoverished and dysfunctional family. His parents fought constantly; to escape the toxic atmosphere, he began spending as much time as possible wandering neighborhood streets in search of diversion. He found it in the act of committing petty larcenies. At age 13, he was arrested for breaking into an apartment building and was soon sent away to a correctional facility.

Once back home, his penchant for committing small thefts resurfaced and he was again sent away again, this time to the St. Bede Academy in downstate Illinois. While there, Heirens excelled in the classroom, displaying a high degree of natural intelligence. He was accepted into a special program at the prestigious University of Chicago and began the term once returning home in 1945. He was now 16.

Heirens proved quite popular with classmates, and was remembered by one girl in the following way: "I remember the most popular boy in my class who was handsome, smart and a good dancer." Apparently however, his academic and social successes were not enough to overcome his addiction to larceny. He continued to look for homes to break into and burgle.

Beginning in June 1945, three Chicago murders, all involving home invasion, took place in fairly rapid succession— and it was these three crimes that the authorities would later link to William Heirens.

Josephine Ross Apartment
4108 N. Kenmore Avenue, Chicago IL 60613

June 5: A 43-year-old woman named Josephine Ross was found dead in her Uptown apartment. She had been repeatedly stabbed and her head was wrapped in a dress. Dark hairs were found in her clutched hands, indicating she had fought for her life. Police surmised she had been surprised by an intruder. No valuables seemed to have been removed from the home.

Frances Brown Apartment
3941 N. Pine Grove, Chicago IL 60613 (Unit 611)

December 10: The naked body of 32-year-old Frances Brown was discovered slumped over her bathtub in her north side apartment. He had been shot in the head and stabbed. A butcher's knife had been driven through her neck. Like Josephine Ross, Brown's head was wrapped, this time in a towel. Also like the Ross crime, no valuables seem to have been taken. Investigators this time did discover a telling clue : a smudged, bloody fingerprint on a door jamb.

Taking a page from Jack the Ripper himself, who had left a chalked message for police during his "Autumn of Terror' killing spree in 1888, Brown's killer had used her lipstick to scrawl this plea on her wall:

For heavens
Sake catch me
Before I kill more
I cannot control myself

The perpetrator was quickly dubbed, "The Lipstick Killer."

The Degnan Home
5943 N. Kenmore Avenue, Chicago IL 60660

January 7, 1946: Around 7:30 AM, James Degnan discovered that his six-year-old daughter, Suzanne, was missing from their Edgewater home.

The police were quickly notified and arrived at the two-story home. A ladder was found leaning against the window to Suzanne's first-floor bedroom, where a ransom note was discovered. An exhaustive canvas of the neighborhood was immediately launched.

The note soon proved to be a cruel ruse. A mysterious, anonymous tip was phoned in to the police, suggesting they search the sewers in the area. Within 12 hours the girl's dismembered body parts began to be discovered deposited nearby.

The first was discovered floating in a sewer catch basin behind an apartment building only a block from her home. Still more body parts would be discovered in other nearby neighborhood sewers. I have listed a few below. You can look up the other locations online if you are so inclined.

5860 N. Kenmore Avenue Chicago IL 60660.

1040 W. Ardmore Avenue, Chicago IL 60660 (NW corner of Kenmore Avenue and Ardmore Avenue).

5907 N. Kenmore Avenue, Chicago IL 60660 (in the alley behind this building).

During their intense canvas of the neighborhood, police discovered a laundry tub, with pipes containing blood, in the basement of a nearby apartment building. It was evident that the killer of Suzanne Degnan had transported her body (she probably was already dead) here for dismemberment.

The Dismemberment Site (basement of this building)
5901—03 N. Winthrop Avenue, Chicago IL 60660

The beleaguered Chicago Police Department was now dealing with three horrific, unsolved north side murders (the latest involving a six year old victim) and was under intense pressure from an outraged public demanding action.

On June 16, 1946, a neighborhood local observed 17-year-old William Heirens breaking into a Rogers Park apartment building and notified authorities. When the police arrived, Heirens pulled a gun and attempted to escape. One officer managed to throw three flowerpots against his head, rendering him unconscious. He was arrested and quickly subjected to an intense interrogation.

The cops weren't interested in a burglar – they were after a killer. The teenager was subjected to a host of brutal "sweating" techniques (a Chicago police specialty of the times) that would no longer be allowed in modern law enforcement. After days of this, they managed to extract a confession for the three crimes. The police would claim that their suspect began to speak of an alter-ego personality—"George Murman"—that was the entity really responsible for the crimes. Heirnes would later claim that all this was merely a ploy; he had only confessed to save his life.

Heirens was soon tried, convicted, and sent off to serve a prison sentence that would last till his death, over 65 years later.

Was William Heirens guilty or innocent of the three murders he was accused of? It's hard to envision ever getting a definitive answer. There are—even today—conflicting opinions.

The Guilty Argument:
1. Heirens was a known burglar who specialized in breaking into homes.
2. He lived relatively close to all three murder locations.
3. The fingerprint found at the Frances Brown murder site, at first denied by police to be Heirens, was later claimed to be his.
4. Heirens signed off on a confession.
5. Similar crimes following the same M.O. stopped after his arrest.

The Innocence Argument:

1. Heirens previous troubles with the law did not reflect any instances of violence.

2. The fingerprint evidence found at the Frances Brown murder site was sketchy at best; it never met several of the FBI-required points to be considered an exact match.

3. The scrawled message on Brown's wall did not appear to resemble Hereins' handwriting.

4. His confession was only signed after several days of brutal police interrogation, including sleep deprivation, "truth serum" injections, and even a forced spinal tap.

Heirens, only 17 at the time, was assured by the authorities that they had solid and conclusive proof against him and the only way for him to avoid the electric chair was to sign a confession.

Heirens would later recant his confession, and claim to the end of his life that he was innocent.

Note: William Heirens died in prison on March 5, 2012, having served a sentence of over 65 years.

Note: If Heirens was indeed guilty of the Ross, Brown & Degnan murders, a serial killer historical precedent, again involving Jack the Ripper, may be instructive.

In 1888, the infamous Ripper murdered at least five women in London's East End. The level of mutilations on his victims increased with each crime save one (most crime historians believe he was interrupted while dispatching Victim #3).

His last "canonical" murder, of a young prostitute named Mary Kelly, was mind-numbingly horrific: Kelly's body was butchered virtually beyond recognition. This would suggest that the Ripper had finally decided that only the total eradication of another human being could satisfy his inner demons.

If William Heirens was guilty, the pattern of an escalating need for ever-greater stimulation at the expense of victims parallels the Ripper case.

Suzanne Degnan's Grave
All Saints Catholic Cemetery
700 N. River Road, Des Plaines IL 60016.
Section 3, Block 8, Lot 2, Grave 3

Heirens's Home
4175 W. Touhy Avenue, Lincolnwood IL 60712
   He lived here at the time of the crimes.

Heirens's Attempted Breakin
6928 N. Wayne, Chicago IL 60626
   A neighbor observed Heirens attempting to burglarize a 3rd floor apartment here on June 26, 1946.

Where Heirens Was Arrested
1320 W. Farwell, Chicago IL 60626
   Arriving police arrested Heirens here.

Eddie Gein:
Honorary Monster of the Midway

   Eddie Gein was not a homicidal product of the Chicagoland area and a visit to his Central Wisconsin home turf requires embarking on a sizeable road trip (approximately 225 miles), but his significant standing in the pantheon of American serial killers makes the journey a must-see.

   Everyone knows the name "Norman Bates," the outwardly normal, yet profoundly disturbed, young homicidal maniac star of Alfred Hitchcock's classic film, *Psycho*. But most people don't realize that Norman Bates was actually based on a real-life Wisconsin man, whose very real macabre deeds made his fictional counterpart seem like Mary Poppins by comparison.

   Ed Gein is the patron saint of disturbed psycho murderers—the ultimate boogeyman. There are two solid reasons:

   1. His mind-numbingly horrific activities, which came to light in 1957s rural Midwest heartland, would send the entire nation into a state of shock, disbelief and revulsion. Americans

simply could not comprehend that another human being, living right in their midst, was capable of deeds so unspeakably perverted they almost defied description—and avoid suspicion for over a decade.

2. Eddie Gein wore, unwittingly, the perfect mask to cover his profound insanity. He was a familiar, somewhat hapless figure in his Plainfield, Wisconsin, town, getting by as the local handyman. He was universally regarded by the community as a good-natured, shy fellow; a bit simple-minded, perhaps, but always ready to chat, help out with a chore or two—or even babysit. To the men of Plainfield, he was the easy butt of jokes, but many housewives secretly felt sorry for him.

Ed Gein was born in 1906 in La Crosse, Wisconsin, the youngest son of George and Augusta Gein. His brother, Henry, was five years older. George was an unambitious alcoholic, who constantly struggled to provide for his family. At the opposite extreme was mother Augusta, the highly-dominant parent, who ruled the family with an iron fist. She belittled and humiliated her husband constantly for his shortcomings and perceived lack of ambition. She was also a full-blown religious zealot, although she believed mostly in her own rigid convictions, based on her personal fiery interpretations of the Bible.

Convinced that LaCrosse was no more than a modern-day Sodom and Gomorrah—(ever been to LaCrosse, Wisconsin?)—she uprooted the family to Plainfield, a small, decidedly bland community in the central portion of the state. There the family purchased a small farm six miles west of town, and began eking out a hardscrabble existence.

If La Crosse was a perverse and sinful city, Plainfield wasn't much better, according to Augusta Gein. The women there were all whores, she declared. The men lowlife scoundrels always attempting to cheat her. She forbade Henry and Ed to have any dealings with fellow townspeople, including schoolmates, if it could be avoided. Thus, Henry and Ed grew up in a profoundly isolated environment. They might as well have spent their formative years on the moon.

Their one source of entertainment, such as it was, was provided by their mother. At night, Augusta would sit the boys at her knee before the fireplace (the farmhouse was not supplied with electricity) and inculcate their young minds with her own, feverish Bible readings. At every opportunity, she would rail against the iniquities of the female sex and stress the hell fires awaiting any man who surrendered to their blandishments. She made her sons swear to her that they would forever avoid women at all costs.

Brother Henry was emotionally strong enough to withstand Augusta's diatribes, as well as the enforced isolation of existence on the farm. For young Ed Gein, conditions proved a perfect breeding ground for blooming insanity.

Life on the Gein farm went on this way for years. It wasn't long before George's influence, under Augusta's withering verbal abuse, had diminished him almost completely. The boys watched as their father was reduced to a virtual non-entity in his own home. He would die suddenly in 1940. For all intents and purposes, it hardly mattered. Soon, another death in the family would occur.

The Gein farm had never been profitable, even in the best of times, and now more income was needed. Henry and Ed began hiring out as handymen and day laborers to their neighbors, although they continued to maintain the farm.

On May 16, 1944, they were burning away vegetation on the property when the fire got out of control. In the smoke and confusion, they became separated. Ed ran to get help. Although he claimed to have no information on his brother's whereabouts, he led rescuers directly to the spot where Henry lay dead. It was noticed that Henry had several injuries to his head, but these were attributed to having occurred when he struck his head while collapsing. The death was labeled an accident.

Now Ed had exactly what he may have always wanted: his mother all to himself. But things soon changed. In 1945, Augusta had a debilitating stroke. Ed devoted himself to taking care of her. Another stroke resulted in her death on December 29, 1945. Neighbors would later recall that Gein wept like a child at her funeral.

Eddie Gein was now all alone in the world.

With Augusta gone, the farmhouse quickly deteriorated. Ed, after sealing off his mother's room as a kind of shrine, reduced his living quarters to the kitchen and one bedroom. Garbage piled up everywhere and no attempt was made to clean or maintain the sagging property. When not busy performing handyman chores in Plainfield or on surrounding farms, Gein devoted himself to reading. His choices in literature were telling: medical texts; true detective magazines; and accounts of bizarre crimes, South Sea cannibals, Nazi atrocities, and the occult.

Virtually shut off from the world in his decaying farmhouse, the years of his mother's preaching, combined with his complete isolation, loneliness, and immersion in bizarre reading materials sent Ed Gein's already tenuous grip on reality over the edge. He became convinced he could raise his mother from the dead. He decided to visit the graveyard where she was buried, exhume her body, and resuscitate it. He would be unsuccessful. Augusta Gein's grave was overlaid with a sheet of concrete too hard to break through.

Gein, although unable to bring his mother back home, soon decided that perhaps replacements would do. Keeping a close eye on the death notices of local women in the obituary sections of newspapers, he began visiting the Plainfield Cemetery (and others in the area) in the dead of night following their funerals. Digging down through the soil in the glow of a lantern, he would smash loose a section of a casket and remove either an entire corpse or a portion of one. He would then carefully rearrange the grave. The remains would be loaded in his truck and transported back to his lonely farmhouse on the edge of town. He would now have company, for at least a while. As the bodies decayed, he began to experiment with different ways to preserve portions of them as personal trophies.

His grave-robbing activities would go on unnoticed for years. But in 1954, he went even further. On December 8 of that year, Mary Hogan, a local tavern owner, who was said to closely resemble Augusta Gein, went missing. Authorities were stumped; the woman seemed to have vanished into thin air. A local man would later report that Eddie Gein had joked about the disappearance with him. When the man wondered where she was, Eddie had insisted she hadn't disappeared at all—she was "back at the house."

November 16, 1957, was the first day of deer hunting in Wisconsin. It was a foregone conclusion among the inhabitants of Plainfield that every able-bodied man in the community would be out in the woods, searching for the first buck of the season.

With the town virtually deserted, Eddie Gein paid a visit to the Worden Hardware Store. Inside, owner Bernice Worden, 58, greeted him, probably somewhat unenthusiastically. Gein had been hanging around the store a lot recently, pestering her for a date. Still, she filled his order for antifreeze and took a .22 rifle down the rack when he expressed a desire to examine it. As she turned to look out the large window fronting Main Street, Gein popped a cartridge into the rifle, took aim, and shot her through the head. He then loaded her body into his truck behind the store and drove off.

Bernice Worden's son, Frank, arrived at the store at 5 PM and found bloodstains on the floor and a rifled cash register.

The police quickly responded to his frantic call. When they asked Frank if he had any suspicions, he immediately mentioned Eddie Gein's name, explaining that the little handyman had been recently bothering his mother. Two officers set off for the Gein farm, six miles west of town.

Darkness had set in as they arrived at the farmhouse. No one answered their knock at the front door, so the men went around to the back of the house, where a rear door led into a summer kitchen/shed. Forcing it open, they switched on flashlights and entered. The shed was pitch black.

As they stumbled around in the darkness, playing their flashlight beams over a jumbled assortment of farm equipment, tools, moldering cardboard boxes and broken furniture, one officer brushed up against an object hanging down from the rafters.

He turned and swung the flashlight beam up; his first thought was that the object was a freshly-killed deer, gutted and partially butchered. Then, time seemed to stand still as his brain struggled to reject what his eyes were showing him. Comprehension slowly dawned. The body hanging before him was not a deer—it was a human female (soon identified as Bernice Worden). It hung down from the rafters from the heels, decapitated and disemboweled. Her head would later be found hidden beneath a decaying mattress.

Lurching away from the horror, the two officers stumbled out into the moonlit yard and fell to their knees, vomiting.

A fleet of police squad cars soon descended on the Gein farm. Ed was quickly located at a neighbor's farm, where he had been invited for dinner. He was thrown into the back of a police car and questioned. At first feigning ignorance about the disappearance of Bernice Worden, he at last whispered the curious comment: "I was framed."

While Ed Gein was being driven to police headquarters, officers entered the main farmhouse. They entered a charnel house of unbelievable horrors. It was sickeningly clear that their shy and reclusive little neighbor had been living a nightmarish existence—and had been for years. While all but two rooms had been closed off, the kitchen and bedroom were a testament to sheer insanity.

Here are a few of the grisly finds:

• Masks created from the stripped flesh from human faces. One of these was so well preserved that officers recognized it as the face of tavern owner, Mary Hogan, who had vanished three years previously.

• Furniture upholstered with human flesh.

• A box containing female genitalia, brightly painted and tied with ribbons.

• A belt composed of female nipples.

• Soup bowls made from skulls.

• A window sash fashioned from human lips

Perhaps the most horrific of all: an upper bodysuit, created from the skins of human females, stitched carefully together, and attached to elastic bands. Gein would later admit that he occasionally donned this death costume and danced in the moonlight.

Ed Gein would finally reluctantly admit killing Mary Hogan and Bernice Worden, but claimed he was "in a daze" at the times. The police already knew this; it was what he told them next that ramped their understanding of his depraved activities up to an entirely new level.

Gein admitted that he had obtained the body parts used for his "decorations" from local graveyards. Exhumations were soon ordered to see if he was telling the truth. He was.

The Plainfield community was stunned and horrified, and to this day, it has never fully recovered. Many of their departed loved ones had wound up as decorations in the house of a madman.

Eddie Gein went to trial, was judged insane, and was sent off to a mental institution for life. He died on July 26, 1984. In death, he got what he had always wanted: to be reunited with his mother. He is buried beside her (in an unmarked grave) at the Plainfield Cemetery—where many of his victims lie.

Ed Gein's Farm
N5691 2nd Avenue, Plainfield WI 54966
SW corner of Archer & 2nd Avenue 54966
The farmhouse house is gone. It "mysteriously" burned down in 1958, shortly after it was announced that it would be opened as an attraction for the curious. Trees have been planted to cover the area, and "No Trespassing" signs are posted everywhere.

Worden's Hardware Store
SE corner of Main Street & North Street, Plainfield WI 54966
The building remained a hardware site for many years afterward, but as of October 2019, it was on the market.

Plainfield Cemetery
N6590 5th Avenue, Plainfield WI 54966
Eddie Gein, his family members, and several victims lie buried here. Ed's grave is unmarked, but it's not all that hard

to identify. Hint: to whom would he want to be closest?

Note: The Plainfield community has been doggedly trying to forget Eddie Gein for over 60 years now, so asking townsfolk about him is not recommended.

4. MURDER & MAYHEM

The "Big 4"
Child Murders that
Changed Chicago Forever

In the years 1955-1957 there were four murders involving children in the Chicagoland area that changed the entire fabric of the up-to-then peaceful neighborhood rhythms of the post-war Windy City, and turned everything upside down– forever. I remember the time well. Doors never before locked were now being carefully locked, kid curfews (usually only laxly enforced) were now strictly mandated, and the admonition, "Don't talk to strangers," became an unceasing mantra uttered incessantly by mothers to any kid within hearing range.

#1. The Peterson-Schuessler Murders: 1955

Note: This one has always fascinated me for a number of reasons.

First, it happened in an area just beyond the outer fringes of what was to become my boyhood stomping ground. Now, since I was only seven years old when the murders took place, my stomping area was admittedly somewhat limited at the time; probably encompassing a one or two block radius from my home in the Belmont-Central neighborhood. But still …

On Sunday, October 16, 1955, three Northwest side boys (Bobby Peterson,14, John Schuessler, 13, Anton Schuessler , Jr.,

The Schuessler/Peterson lonely dump site on Lawrence Avenue.

11), set off to see a movie in downtown Chicago. They never returned home.

Two days later, on October 18, their lifeless, naked bodies were found discarded in a ditch at the Robinson Woods Forest Preserve, about 10 miles west from their homes.

The case baffled authorities (in large part because of their own bungled investigation) for more than 35 years. In 1991, investigators looking into the 1977 Helen Brach disappearance (another cold case covered later in this book) received a tip regarding the Peterson-Schuessler murders.

A source connected to the shady Chicagoland "Equestrian Mafia" (a group of unscrupulous stable owners involved in a host of unsavory activities) revealed that a man named Kenneth Hansen, also a figure in the group, had bragged several times over the years about having killing three boys in 1955 — and getting away with it.

Hansen was soon charged with the crime and convicted in 1995. During the trial, prosecutors laid out the following timeline based on evidence and eyewitness testimonies :

1. The Schuessler brothers left their home *(5711 N. Mango Avenue, Chicago, IL 60646)* and biked to Bobby Peterson's *(5519*

N. Farragut Avenue, Chicago IL 60630).

2. The 3 boys set off shortly after 3 PM for *the Oriental The-atre in downtown Chicago* to see the Disney film, African Lion.

3. Despite admonitions from their parents to return di-rectly home after the movie, the boys decided to go bowling. A teenage acquaintance briefly chatted with them at the *Monte Cristo Bowl (3326 W. Montrose Avenue, Chicago IL 60618).*

4. After leaving the Monte Cristo, which was fully booked up, the boys headed west in a now-falling drizzle. They made their way to another bowling establishment, the *Drake Bowl (3550 W. Montrose Avenue, Chicago IL 60618)*, only to find that all 16 lanes there were also booked up for the night. A manager spotted them there around 8 PM.

It is at this point that things get decidedly odd. The boys were not rebellious by nature. They were not prone to disobey-ing their parents. It was now dark and damp—and long after the time they were expected home. Things were about to get even stranger.

5. Bobby, John and Anton were next seen just after 9 PM by a motorist on the *southeast corner of Lawrence Avenue and Mil-waukee Avenue (approx. 4787 N. Milwaukee Avenue 60630)*, across from the Hoyne Bank Building, which still stands today. Their parents, at home, were now growing frantic with worry.

Here is what police theorized happened next:

6. Kenneth Hansen, a 22- year-old stable hand who worked at the *Idle Hour Stables (located at Higgins and River Road)*, pulled up in his car to this intersection. He somehow convinced the boys to accompany him to the stables, ostensibly to show them some prize horses. Hanson had used this tactic many times before.

At his 1995 trial, former co-workers testified that he was a known pedophile and had often lured other young men to the Idle Hour under the very same pretext. At least one former sta-ble hand also claimed that Hansen had boasted over the years about his involvement in the Peterson-Schuessler murders.

It's here that things begin to get really murky. The three boys *had* to have known that they were already in deep trouble with their parents. *Why* would they have compounded their

All that's left today of the Idle Hour Stables.

troubles by going with Hansen? Were they physically coerced? Was Hansen alone? Unfortunately, we will never know.

7. Hansen transported the three boys to the Idle Hour Stables, located on Higgins Road. After sending Bobby and John off to another area of the property, he accosted Anton in a barn. Unexpectedly, the two older boys returned and found Hansen in the act. Both boys, Bobby in particular, went ballistic and threatened to tell their parents. Hansen, panicked, grabbed Bobby and struck him on the head over and over with the first stable implement he could reach.

8. The three boys were quickly strangled to death. Bobby Peterson's later autopsy would show that he had been struck repeatedly on the head. Authorities believed that he had most likely been the first to die.

Someone else had to have become involved at this point; it's unreasonable to assume that one man could have dispatched three boys single-handedly. Who was it? Still unknown. Perhaps another stable hand who will forever evade justice.

9. Kenny Hansen now had three dead bodies on his hands. He needed help in covering up the crime and called in reinforcements. The most logical candidate: his brother, Curtis Hansen, a violent man who was a greatly-feared figure in the 'equestrian mafia'. He had bailed his brother out of trouble on numerous occasions. And it is virtually impossible that the owner of the Idle Hour Stable, the notorious Silas Jayne (see The Strange Case of the Candy Lady), remained unaware of the happenings on his property. He, too, might have likely arrived soon. Reportedly, he was furious.

10. Kenneth Hansen, Curtis, and possibly Jayne stripped the bodies of their clothing undoubtedly to eliminate evidence, disposed of it (the clothing was never found), and loaded the bodies into a vehicle. They were then transported a few miles southwest, where they were discarded hastily and haphazardly into a ditch at the Robinson Woods Forest Preserve:

Robinson Woods Forest Preserve. Lawrence Avenue, between East River Road & River Road, Chicago IL 60706.

🔎 *Note:* The bodies were found approximately 200 feet south of the Lawrence Avenue entrance, in the ditch on the east side of the drive.

11. The bodies of the three boys would be discovered on Tuesday, October 18th. A bungled investigation produced no results. On May 15, 1956, a barn on the property of Silas Jaynes' Idle Hour Stables mysteriously burned down, conveniently eliminating a source of possible evidence.

🔎 *Note:* As noted previously, this case remained "cold" for decades. When an informant revealed new information to police investigating the disappearance of Helen Brach (1991), they began to take a fresh look at Kenneth Hansen and his boasts regarding the 1956 murders. He would wind up being convicted of the Schuessler-Peterson crimes and dying in prison in 2007 (maintaining his innocence to the end), but it is virtually a certainty that if he truly was the killer, he had accomplices who ultimately avoided punishment.

🔍 *Note:* Anton Schuessler, Sr., father of John and Anton, Jr., was a fourth victim of the events. He died of a massive heart attack, no doubt brought on by anguish and grief, less than a month after the murders.

Idle Hour Stables. 8600 Higgins Road, Chicago IL 60631. As Chicago continued to expand over the years, this entire area was subjected to intensive redevelopment. Most of the land, once open fields and riding trails, lies now beneath a vast sea of concrete. A hotel parking lot covers most of the area to the south of Higgins. The north side, where most of Idle Hour's stables and outbuildings once stood, is now an array of businesses, including a large food market. Two small, white-washed wooden structures remain tucked into a back corner of the property, untouched by time. They appear to be all that's left of the Idle Hour Stables.

🔍 *Note:* The clothes of the three murdered boys were never found. It is a distinct possibility that Bobby's White Sox jacket and John and Anton's blue satin Cubs jackets lie forever buried beneath all that concrete.

Schuessler Graves: John, Anton, Jr. and Anton Sr. St. Joseph Cemetery, 3100 N. Thatcher Avenue, River Grove IL 60171 Section L, Lot 237.

🔍 *Note:* As noted previously, John and Anton's dad, Anton, Sr., would join the boys here within weeks. The stress of the tragedy resulted in a massive heart attack. He died on November 11, 1955.

Bobby Peterson Grave: Rosehill Cemetery, 5800 N. Ravenswood Avenue, Chicago IL 60660, Plot 119, Lot 31, Sub Plot 1.

🔍 *Note:* For decades, amateur sleuths have been trying to link the Peterson-Schuessler murders to the following crime. The evidence, however, is just not there.

#2 : The Grimes Girls: 1956
The Chicagoland area, still reeling from the Peterson-Schuessler murders in 1955, were again blindsided the following year by another horrific child-murder case; one eerily reminiscent of it. Sisters Patricia and Barbara Grimes, aged 15 and 12, vanished on a night in December, 1956. Their frozen and naked bodies would be found beside the bridge embankment of a lonely suburban road just over three weeks later. Unlike the Peterson-Schuessler case, finally resolved after decades, these murders remain unsolved to this very day.

The Grimes sisters were huge fans of Elvis Presley. Three days after Christmas, on December 28, they persuaded their mother, Loretta, to allow them permission to attend a screening of Presley's film, *Love Me Tender*, at the nearby Brighton Theater — even though they had already seen it several times. They promised to be home before midnight.

The probable timeline of events, determined by police:

1. Barbara and Patricia left their home on Damon Avenue at approximately 7:30 PM, bound for the Brighton Theater, a few miles SW.

2. At the Brighton, they were seen by and interacted with several school acquaintances, who will later state that the girls seemed in good spirits and untroubled. They stay for a second screening of the film, which would still allow them enough time to make it back home by 11:45 PM.

3. Several witnesses will later claim they had seen the Grimes sisters conversing with a young male resembling Elvis Presley outside the theater.

4. Mrs. Grimes began to get very concerned when the girls had not returned home by midnight, and sent two other of her children to the nearest bus stop to wait for them. No luck. At 2:15 AM she placed a call to police to file a missing person report.

5. Authorities, with the Peterson-Schuessler case fresh on their minds, conducted an exhaustive investigation/search for the girls. A confusing array of leads emerged: reports that the

A lonely stretch of German Church Road: the Grimes girls' 1956 dump site.

girls have been seen in a variety of Chicago locations, claims they have they moved in with older boyfriends, even theories they have run away to Tennessee to visit Elvis.

Presley himself will issue the following plea to the girls on January 19: "If you are good Presley fans, you'll go home and ease your mother's worries."[10]

None of these leads seems to align with the characteristic behavior patterns of Barbara and Patricia.

6. On January 22, 1957, a construction worker traveling along German Church Road, in Willow Springs notices two mannequin-like figures sprawled bedside a guard rail approximately 200 yards east of County Line Road. A recent thaw had melted the snow cover in the area.

Police quickly arrived and identified the bodies of Barbara and Patricia Grimes.

7. A plethora of confusing information on autopsy reports and theories emerges, largely caused by incompetent investigative techniques and political meddling. Even the specific cause of death failed to be determined. The official conclusion:

death by exposure).

Several suspects were apprehended, investigated and later released.

The crimes remain unsolved.

🔍 *Note:* A few salient points:

a. The most reliable autopsy information reveals that the Grimes sisters died within five hours of their last known sighting at the Brichton Theater. Despite obvious body wounds to the victims (the coroner decided they were rodent bites), several shallow stab-like indentations on Barbara's chest are instructive.

b. Loretta Grimes, the girls' mother, received several disturbing telephone calls after the murders. One anonymous caller not only claimed responsibility for the killings, he related a fact about Barbara that only her killer would know: the toes on one of her feet were crossed.

This same caller (Loretta Grimes swore she recognized his voice) phoned her again in the fall of 1958 to claim he had committed another perfect crime for which he would escape punishment. On the previous day, the nude, decapitated body of a teenage girl had been found in a nearby forest preserve.

c. The Grimes girls' case has a definite link to the 1958 Bonnie Leigh Scott case, which will be explored in just a bit.

Barbara & Patricia Grimes' Home. 3634 S. Damen Avenue, Chicago IL 60609. It's still there, although considerably remodeled.

Brighton Theater. 4223 S. Archer Avenue, Chicago, IL 60632. Long gone. Just an empty lot now. Barbara and Patricia were seen here by several friends.

The Grimes Girls' Dump Site. German Church Road. (Just East of) County Line Road, Burr Ridge IL 60527. Look for a guard rail overlooking a creek. The surrounding area is much different today from the way it was in late 1956. The housing developments are all recent. Back then, this would have been a remote

On the night of August 16, 1957, 15-year-old Judith Mae Anderson headed home down this Central Avenue Block. She never made it.

and secluded area.

The Graves of the Grimes Girls. Holy Sepulchre Cemetery, 6072 W. 111th St., Alsip IL 60415. Section 37, Lot 21, Block 8.

#3 : Judith Mae Anderson: 1957

On August 16, 1957, 15-year-old Judith Mae Anderson left her N. Lotus Avenue home to walk the short distance to visit a friend, Elena Abbatacola.

Judith Mae Anderson Home. 1529 N. Lotus Avenue, Chicago, IL 60651.

Elena Abbatacola Home. 1019 N. Central, Chicago IL 60651 (2nd story apartment).

The two girls ventured out for a quick visit to a nearby dairy bar before returning to Elena's house for a night of television viewing. Around 11 PM, Judith phoned her mother to ask permission to stay just a bit longer, but the request was denied. Elena volunteered to accompany her at least halfway home, but Judith declined the offer, assuring her there was no need. She would be just fine. Judith Mae Anderson set off for home into the summer night and was not seen alive again.

By 12 PM Judith's father, Ralph, was growing very concerned. He called the Abbatacola's, but there was no answer. He then scoured the neighborhood before driving to the Abbatacola home, awakening the family. They could provide little help, only that Judith had mentioned she would be taking a bus toward home.

At 3:25 AM, Ralph Anderson called the police to report a missing daughter.

On Thursday, August 22, boaters at Montrose Harbor spotted a 55-gallon drum floating offshore. When they pulled it ashore and opened it, they found the torso of a young female. Her head, an arm, and the opposite hand were missing. Their immediate thought was it had belonged to a young woman in her 20s.

On Saturday, August 24, another drum, this one only five gallons, was pulled from the harbor. It was found to contain a head, an arm, and a hand.

Montrose Harbor. 601 W. Montrose Avenue, Chicago IL 60613. Now the authorities had enough information to make a positive identification. Through dental records and fingerprints, they determined the victim was 15-year-old Judith Mae Anderson. She had been shot in the head four times with a .32 caliber handgun. The sloppy and inefficient nature of her dismemberment, in which a knife, hacksaw and hatchet had all been used, led police to the conclusion that her killer was inexperienced. Today, he would probably also be tagged "disorganized." This conclusion was reinforced by his method of body disposal. Choosing a popular lake front area, frequented at all times by fishermen and boaters, was risky.

In fact, the one clue authorities gleaned in the case was provided by a local harbor fisherman, who reported observing an odd event a few nights earlier. A car, with brake light flashing, backed slowly down to the water's edge. A well-built man had exited the vehicle, opened the trunk, and tossed several large items into the water. The darkness prevented a more complete description but a crucial detail was provided: one of the car's taillights was out.

The investigation intensity ramped up. In addition to the search for the man responsible for the gruesome Judith Mae Anderson murder, the police had also been on the hunt for a man who had committed a string of sexual assaults on women in the north side Chicago area. In these cases, the woman were confronted while walking alone, frequently after hopping off buses. The perpetrator used a knife to stab at the women, frequently aiming for the genital area. Curiously, none of the victims were subjected to rape.

The police now upped their presence on the street. Many officers began trailing city buses at discreet distances. Soon a break appeared: a car was observed doggedly following a bus on Western Avenue near Peterson. The car had a broken taillight. These two facts gave the cops a solid reason to pull the car over.

At the wheel was a 21-year-old truck driver named Barry Zander Cook, who closely fit the physical descriptions provided by victims. The police officers were quite aware of the significance of their stop, but they did not want to arouse Cook's suspicions. They simply took his information, wrote out a ticket for the broken taillight and sent him off. When a background check revealed that he had a previous arrest record, antennas really went up.

The next step for the authorities was to covertly arrange for female victims to observe Barry Cook in person. To that end, they were brought to construction sites where he was working.

All went smoothly until February 6, 1958, when he recognized a woman pointing him out and attempted to flee the scene. He was apprehended by detectives, receiving a gunshot wound to the leg in the process. Brought to an area hospital for treatment, it was discovered that Cook had the genitalia of a six-year-old boy and so was unable to achieve normal sexual gratification.

While in the hospital, Cook refused any form of cooperation with authorities, often feigning unconsciousness, and only speaking with this father. During this time, victims were brought to his hospital room in the attempt to identify their assailant.

As a result of their positive identifications, Cook was soon charged with seven counts of assault. He would eventually be sent off to Joliet penitentiary to serve a 14-year sentence.

Because of the nature of the crimes, police were now beginning to link their suspect to the Judith Mae Anderson case, as well as a yet-unsolved 1956 murder.

On July 23 of that year, a female sunbather named Margaret Gallagher had been attacked and slain in Lincoln Park, not far from the spot where Judith Anderson's remains had been found. A resident at a nearby high rise had actually observed the attack through binoculars but had been unable to provide a clear description of the killer.

Barry Cook remained uncooperative with authorities, still insisting on talking only with his father. The elder Cook was, however, persuaded that a polygraph examination could clear his son's name, and he agreed to allow it. His son failed it miserably; the test showed that he had inside information about both the Gallagher and Anderson murders. After the test, Cook admitted to a detective that he had indeed killed Judith Anderson.

All progress in clearing up the cases immediately screeched to a halt when Cook's father became re-involved, instructing Barry to refuse to communicate further with anyone besides him.

While Cook was back in jail, authorities planted an undercover agent, posing as a fellow prisoner, in his cell. Befriending the suspect, the agent soon learned a lot; in fact, Cook freely admitted to the slayings and provided detailed accounts of how he had carried them out.

When later confronted by detectives and told of the information they now had, Cook asked to speak to the prison warden. He now fully confessed to the murder of Margaret

Gallagher.

Despite the wealth of evidence, Barry Cook was astound-ingly acquitted of the murder charge in his subsequent trial; the jury believed the testimony of his parents, who claimed he had been home with them at the time of the murder.

Although shocked and dismayed by the turn of events, the police were not ready to throw in the towel on nailing a man they were convinced was guilty of at least two murders; they doubled down on their efforts to tie Barry Cook to the Judith Mae Anderson case. Detectives managed to enter the Cook home while the family was out of town. In the basement, they found flattened .32 caliber slugs, the same type that were found in Judith Anderson's body.

By the use of eavesdropping devices, they also learned that Cook's father had discovered a revolver beneath the front porch and buried it on the property—somewhere, he told Barry, it would never be found. In addition, shortly after the Judith Anderson murder, the Cook family had arranged for a cement foundation to be poured over a portion of the back-yard, ostensibly for a barbecue pit. Authorities wondered if the girl's clothing, which was never found, now lay beneath the concrete.

The police could never definitively pin Barry Zander Cook to the Judith Mae Anderson murder, and he was released from prison in 1967. Upon release, the Cook family relocated to Houston, Texas. There, Cook would be suspected of at least one other violent assault, but he was never formally charged.

Detectives who worked the Chicago Anderson case re-mained firmly convinced Cook had indeed killed Judith Mae Anderson. They believed he had abducted the girl, shot her in his car, transported her to his home for dismemberment, and sealed her body in oil drums before dumping the evidence into Montrose Harbor.

They just couldn't make it stick.

Barry Zander Cook's Home (in 1940). 1767 Granville Avenue, Chicago IL 60660. Okay, I freely admit I need help with this one. My research could only confirm that the Cook family was living here in 1940, but that was years before the Judith Mae Anderson murder. There are tantalizing hints that the family was living in another nearby residence on Hermitage Avenue (near Devon Avenue) at that time, but so far I have been unable to verify the address. Any assistance from the public would be greatly appreciated!

#4 : Bonnie Leigh Scott: 1958

On September 22, 1958, Bonnie Leigh Scott, a 15-year-old girl living in Addison with her aunt, uncle and grandmother, failed to return home. A missing person report was promptly filed with the police, who began an investigation. During interviews with Bonnie's high school friends, they learned that she had a somewhat close relationship with an older man, Charles Leroy Melquist.

Melquist, a 23-year-old masonry worker from Villa Park, proved remarkably open and helpful, not only with the police, but also to Bonnie Leigh's family. He spent several days driving through the surrounding areas with her frantic grandmother on a search for the missing girl. He told authorities that he was really a sort of "big brother" to Bonnie, and advised her on solving her teenage problems. He also claimed that she had called him up on the night of her disappearance, expressing doubts about the boy she was with.

On November 15, a group of Boy Scouts hiking through the nearby Argonne Woods Forest Preserve in Palos Township came upon a gruesome find: the decapitated, naked body of a young girl. The remains were lying near a guard rail, approximately 250 feet south of the intersection of 95th Street and La-Grange Road.

The authorities were now taking a really hard look at Charles Melquist and wanted to bring him in for further questioning. They set off to find him on November 16. Before they could locate him, he voluntarily turned himself in at a nearby police station. While he was being interrogated, the police were examining his car. After his interview, he was allowed to leave; he was told that he was not considered a suspect.

Everything changed when it was determined that evidence gleaned from the car indicated that Bonnie had been murdered in it. Melquist was brought back to the station for another round of questioning. It was noted that his answers seemed somewhat robotic and rehearsed. He was then given a polygraph test, which he failed miserably. Detectives decided to administer a second test at the offices of a noted polygraph expert and drove off with the suspect.

Along the way, they stopped for a meal, during which Melquist confided that he knew "the jog (jig) was up." After failing the second polygraph test, he wrote out a seven-page confession. In it, he stated that he and Bonnie Leigh had been "fooling around" in his car when he "accidentally" smothered her with a pillow. He had then undressed her, and drove around with her dead body until finding a suitable place near the forest preserve to dispose of it.

He also confessed to returning to the dump site at least twice. The first visit was only days after the murder. Melquist claimed he wanted to be sure the body was "still there." Three weeks later, he returned with a pitchfork and large knife. He mutilated and decapitated the corpse. A sick sidenote: during the same time period, he was also escorting Bonnie's frantic grandmother around the area on a "search" for the missing girl. Decidedly heartless.

A search of Melquist's Villa Park home produced a long list of teenage girls' phone numbers—some of whom lived in Barbara and Patricia Grimes' neighborhood. Upon further investigation, many girls would admit to a series of anonymous, harassing calls. In addition, several girls came forward to claim that Melquist had attempted "rough play" on dates– and had even attempted to choke them.

Charles Melquist was soon tried and convicted of the murder of Bonnie Leigh Scott. His defense of being "hypnotized" at the time of the murder did not sit well with the jury. He received a sentence of 99 years. Amazingly, he was released after serving only 11 years. He would go on to marry and father two children. Charles Leroy Melquist died in 2010.

 Note: It's extremely puzzling that authorities did not

make a legitimate connection between the murder of Bonnie Leigh Scott and the Grimes sisters. They were teenage girls. They lived on the Southside of Chicago. The bodies of all three wound up deposited in similar locations, beside a guard rail in wooded areas. Mrs. Grimes received cruel calls after the murders from an anonymous caller claiming to be the killer; Charles Melquist loved making anonymous calls. He was also obsessed with teenage girls. In addition, he was 22-23 years old, a prime age for sexually-driven serial killers.

And—remember those curious indentations on Barbara Grimes' chest? Melquist admitted to police that he had returned to the Bonnie Leigh Scott dump site and inflicted mutilation on her corpse with a knife. This would have taken place, by his own admission, in a September-October time period. Barbara and Patricia Grimes were killed in late December. It was a very cold winter. Their bodies were discovered on January 22, frozen. If Charles Melquist had followed his previous M.O., a visit to the dump site following the murders to inflict further mutilations, he would have been frustrated by the conditions of the bodies. Knife thrusts into frozen flesh would only produce shallow indentations.

And there things rest.

Bonnie Leigh Scott Home. 112 Normandy Drive, Addison IL 60101.

Bonnie Leigh Scott Dump Site. 95th Street and LaGrange Road, Palos Township IL 60465. Bonnie Leigh's body was found just south of here, near a guard rail.

Charles Melquist Home. 655 S. Yale Street, Villa Park IL 60181.

═══ More Murder & Mayhem ═══

"It is my belief, Watson, founded upon my experience, that the lowest and vilest alleys in London do not present a more dreadful record of sin than does the smiling and beautiful countryside."

— Arthur Conan Doyle,
The Adventure of the Copper Beeches

The Patty Columbo Murders: A Rebellious Teen's Revenge

🔍 *Note:* The Columbo Family murder case of 1976 always had much to catch my interest: a compelling mixture of the outre, the horrific, and the downright bizarre. The specifics, including a willful, beautiful teen vixen, her much older Svengali boyfriend, and the bloody massacre of a family seem to be straight out of a noir Hollywood script. As if that weren't enough, the main protagonist, young Patty Columbo, as well as her younger brother/victim, Michael, both attended school in what would one day be the district I would teach in.

Frank and Mary Columbo, not unlike many parents of the time, wanted to raise their two children, Patricia and Michael, away from the street of the big city, and chose the quiet northwest Chicago suburb of Elk Grove Village to settle. Outwardly, theirs was a just a typical suburban family: hardworking dad, involved mom, dutiful kids. But, underneath the surface, trouble was brewing. Patty, now sixteen, always the apple of her father's eye and treated like a princess, was chafing under the bit of parental discipline. She was quickly developing a wild side that was quickly becoming a major source of concern and irritation to her parents.

Patty attracted the interest of a 36-year-old, married (five kids!) pharmacist named Frank DeLuca, who hired her for his Walgreen's pharmacy. The two began a torrid (and quite kinky) love relationship. I won't go into the details. If you really want to know, look it up.

Patty's family members (especially her old-school Italian dad) needless to say, were not exactly thrilled with all this, but there was little they could do to rein in their daughter. Patty soon moved in with DeLuca. For a while, she even lived right in the midst of the whole DeLuca clan, wife and five kids included!

Eventually, DeLuca chose Patty over his family and the

two lovers moved into an apartment in Lombard. This development infuriated and frustrated Frank Columbo. He would soon confront DeLuca in the parking lot of the pharmacy and smash a rifle butt into his jaw, dislodging several teeth, as a warning to end the relationship with his daughter.

This action seemed to now galvanize Patty. According to accounts she began to dominate the relationship with her older boyfriend and began actively seeking out reputed hitmen (actually woefully inept hitmen wannabes) to kill her father.

Not surprisingly, nothing happened. A frustrated Patty finally decided that if she wanted the deed done, she would have to take matters into her own hands. As she formulated her plans, she upped the stakes. Killing her father would both protect her lover from future harm—and allow Patty herself a measure of revenge against her old man for imagined wrongs/discipline punishments of the past. But, if her entire family were eliminated, why, she and DeLuca could inherit a nice bit of money and fuel their future lives together. What Patty didn't know: Frank and Mary Columbo had already written her out of their will.

On the night of May 4, 1976, the doorbell of the Columbo residence rang. Frank Columbo answered the door to find DeLuca, with Patty right behind, training a .32 caliber pistol on him. He turned and raced up a short flight of stairs as DeLuca fired. Collapsing in the living room, he was shot several more times, then bashed repeatedly on the head with a bowling trophy and a lamp.

The later police investigation reported that the back of his head had virtually disintegrated. A startled Mary Columbo emerged from an upstairs bathroom only to receive a bullet between the eyes. As she lay dying, she was beaten with a glass vase and had her throat slashed.

The killers then made their way upstairs to Michael's room. The still half-asleep 13-year-old boy was forced out of bed and shot. A pair of sewing scissors were then used to inflict a host of shallow stab wounds to his body—over 80 of them. The sheer rage behind this brutality would later sicken investigators, and indicate that this crime was personal. The perpetrator here had waged a very personal vendetta against the victim.

The killers' last act in the home was to turn the thermostat up to 97 degrees, apparently to hasten the decomposition of the bodies—and the evidence.

The murders went undiscovered for several days. On May 7, Frank Columbo's car was discovered abandoned on Chicago's West Side. Elk Grove authorities were notified, and they went to the Columbo residence to find a scene of carnage. The stench of rotting flesh was overpowering. Frank Columbo's bloody, decomposing corpse lay in the living room, his teeth scattered across the carpet. Mary Columbo's body was visible on an upstairs landing. Soon Michael's body, so covered in red marks that the responders at first thought he had suffered from a bad case of measles, was discovered upstairs.

Patty Columbo was notified of events at the apartment she shared with Frank DeLuca, and put on a show of surprise, shock and horror, but the police were suspicious from the outset; there was something just not quite right about her performance. In addition, her account of her whereabouts in the days before and after the murders were sketchy. Even more red flags were raised when she began almost immediately to suggest possible theories and motives behind the crimes. As investigators learned more about Frank DeLuca and their relationship, their suspicions deepened. When Patty actually began to flirt with attending police officers at her family's wake and funeral, the spotlight was now firmly shining on the teen and her lover.

Within days, the promise of reward money lured two men to authorities, where they related the attempts by Patty Columbo to hire them to kill her family. The police, now armed with plenty of evidence, arrested Patty on May 15, and charged her with the murders of her family. Frank DeLuca would be taken into custody and charged shortly after.

At their subsequent trials, DeLuca's co-workers would testify that they had observed him burning bloody clothing on the day after the murder and threatened them to keep quiet.

Patty Columbo and Frank DeLuca were convicted of three

counts of murder and received life sentences.

🔍 *Note:* A lead investigator in the case has always believed that DeLuca did the shooting, and Patty inflicted the scissor mutilations. While DeLuca eventually accepted responsibility for his role in the crimes, Patty Columbo has remained coy about it. Both have been repeatedly denied parole over the years.

The Columbo Family Home (and murder site). 55 Brantwood Avenue, Elk Grove Village IL 60007.

Walgreens (where Patty Columbo & Frank DeLuca worked). 930 Town Center, Elk Grove Village IL 60007. This is not the original building. The Walgreens where DeLuca was employed as a pharmacist (and Patty a waitress) was on the south side of this shopping center. Frank Columbo, Patty's father, attacked DeLuca in this parking lot, sparking DeLuca's desire for revenge.

Patty Columbo/Frank DeLuca Apartment (Patty taken into custody here). 2015 S. Findley Road, Lombard IL 60148 (Apt. #911).
Graves of Frank, Mary & Michael Columbo. Windridge Memorial Park, 7014 S. Rawson Bridge Road, Cary IL 60013.

The Rouse Family Murders: Death In The Family
2057 N. Milwaukee Avenue, Libertyville IL 60048
(just north of Buckley Road)

The house is now long gone, burned to the ground in 2002, but the memories of the 1980 horrific murders of millionaires Bruce and Darlene Rouse linger.

On this site once stood the extremely impressive home of an outwardly appearing All-American family. Father Bruce, 44, was a self-made success, whose hard work had paid off (he owned a chain of gas stations, had real estate and cable services interests. He shared the home with his wife, Darlene, 38, and three children: son Kurt, 20, daughter Robin (16) and son Billy (15).

But beneath the surface, trouble was brewing, and it

peaked by June of 1980. Oldest son, Kurt, had frustrated his parents with a lack of career ambition. He lived in a small guesthouse located a few hundred feet behind the main house. Robin was getting along fine with her parents, but often butted heads with Kurt. Youngest child, Billy, presented Bruce and Darlene with their biggest challenge. A troubled kid all his life, he had now turned to alcohol, drugs and vandalism.

On the night of June 5, 1980, a raging thunderstorm struck the area. Inside the Rouse home, an even worse storm was raging. An exasperated Darlene had finally reached her limit that evening when she detected alcohol on Billy's breath. They violently quarreled, with a furious Darlene vowing to send her wayward son to a military school as soon as possible.

This ominous pronouncement, it was later learned, sent the volatile Billy Rouse over the edge.

The next morning, one of Bruce Rouse's employees telephoned the house; Billy picked up the phone. Bruce had not shown up at one of his gas stations (as he always did), and instructions were needed. Billy said he would check with his dad. A minute later, an hysterical-sounding Billy was screaming that his parents had been killed in bed.

The Lake County Police soon arrived at the house to find a horrific scene. The master bedroom was awash with carnage. Blood and brain matter were splattered everywhere. Darlene Rouse had taken a point-blank shotgun blast to the head, killing her instantly. Bruce had also received a blast that had taken off his jaw, but didn't kill him. His killer had finished him off with repeated blows to the head, as well as five stab wounds to the heart.

The most experienced authorities immediately identified the nature of the slayings—the extreme brutality shown by the perpetrator—as pointing to this being a very personal kind of crime, involving a high degree of anger toward the victims. It was quickly determined that nothing of any real value, except several of Mr. Rouse's weapons and a few pieces of jewelry, was missing (these items were soon found in the nearby Des Plaines River). The actual murder weapon, though, was never found.

And all three children claimed to have heard absolutely nothing. (Shotgun blasts?!)

You didn't have to be a Lt. Columbo to smell something a little fishy here—and the cops certainly did. They quickly lasered their sights in on the Rouse siblings. But the kids weren't talking.

And the police just couldn't prove anything.

The kids wound up with healthy inheritances and quickly drifted away from each other. Kurt would move to California. Robin, staying in the area, wound up dying in a car accident in 1983. Billy drifted down to Florida and began drinking away his money; it would soon be gone. A marriage fell apart.

He began getting in trouble with the law for a string of petty crimes. In 1995, his involvement as an accomplice in two south Florida bank robberies got him into considerably more serious trouble. He was quickly apprehended by the Florida police. Upon hearing of his arrest, Illinois authorities decided to fly down to interrogate him a final time about the 1980 murders. This time, and for whatever reasons, Billy was ready to talk.

He confessed to the murders, citing his rage at his mother's constant criticisms of him. According to him, her threat on that June night to send him off to a military school was the straw that broke the camel's back. He would soon be convicted of the crime and sent off to an eighty-year prison sentence. He is serving it still.

But wait—there's more!

You would think that after the events described above, a house like this could not possibly add to its notorious reputation—but that's exactly what happened. Soon after the murders, the house lay empty. The Rouse kids, inheritance money in hand, were gone. The seven-and-a-half-acre property was now on the market, but prospective home seekers were not exactly scrambling to purchase a house already being dubbed "Hell House" by area residents.

There have been many unconfirmed rumors about what happened next. According to one, a county law enforcement official moved in to the house and quickly turned it into a kind of personal playground. Wild parties were thrown, supposedly attended by other law enforcement officials. It was rumored that one of these parties, a costume event, was actually themed around the Rouse murders.

Again (allegedly), word of the goings-on eventually leaked out, scandal ensued, and party time came to a screeching halt.

That's surely the end of the story, right? Wrong.

The house now became the property of the Chicago Outfit, who were looking to expand vice operations deeper into the northern suburbs. The mob chieftains sunk $50,000 into renovations, converting what had been a family home into a combination casino/brothel. And allegedly, county officials turned a blind eye to the vice activities taking place under their noses.

Thankfully, and almost unbelievably, the whole house of cards came tumbling down after only two weeks of operation. A bookmaker, on mob orders, was whacked right on the property. Even though his body was disposed of (placed in the trunk of his car and left in a neighboring suburb), the heat was on for the Outfit.

The vice den was soon closed down and the building itself was eventually demolished to clear the way for a new housing development.

A true suburban Hell House was now gone!

P.S.: I just got back from a re-visit to the site. The grounds of the former seven-and-a-half-acre Rouse estate are now covered by—you guessed it – townhouses, and (to the northwest) single family homes. Every one of them looks like it was constructed about three days ago.

Still, just strolling through the area where notorious events like this took place, as every fan of crime history knows, is pretty cool. I am tempted to say that I heard the sounds of shotgun blasts and ghostly screams in the wind, but I didn't.

So, I won't.

Not far away to the southwest is a small cemetery where Bruce, Darlene—and Robin, in 1983 were laid to rest. If you are so inclined, take a moment to pay your respects.

Graves of Bruce, Darlene & Robin Rouse. Diamond Lake Cemetery (Section 1, Lot 71). 1257 Townline Road (Route 60), Mundelein IL 60060.

The Luettgart Sausage Vat Murder
1735 W. Diversey Parkway, Chicago IL 60614

Do you remember the old saying that goes something like this (and I paraphrase)? "You may love sausage—but you don't want to see how it's made." Well, here's Exhibit A.

Few driving past the intersection of Diversey Parkway and Hermitage Avenue would have even a faint clue today about the dark history of the building on the south side of the street.

Back in 1897, this five-story edifice (now converted to condominiums) was part of the A. L. Luetgert Sausage and Packing Company, owned by Adolph Luegert, the self-proclaimed "Sausage King of Chicago."

Now, old Adolph was a hot-tempered fellow, and often his ire was directed at his second wife, Louisa. It didn't help matters that Mr. Luetgert was fooling around with a family maid, and Louisa knew it. In addition, Luetgert was carrying on an affair with a woman named Christine Feldt, whom he had promised to marry if "something happened" to Louisa.

On the night of May 1, 1897, things seemed to have boiled over, so to speak. On that night, Louisa was seen entering the building with Adolph by a factory worker at around 10:30 PM. And no one ever saw her again. The factory seemed to be working late that night. Smoke was seen pouring out of the smokestack into the early morning hours.

Louisa's disappearance troubled her relatives. Three days after she vanished, they called on Luetgert, who assured them she had traveled north to Wisconsin to visit an aunt. When this explanation proved false, Louisa's worried brother notified the police. When they questioned Luetgert, he changed his story, now claiming she had run off with another man. The police were extremely suspicious and launched an investigation.

Police Captain Herman Schuettler and his men conducted

The old Luettgart Sausage Factory building, now converted into condominiums. Knockwurst, anyone?

a search of the factory. In the basement, they discovered two gold rings, one bearing the initials "L. L." in a large vat. Bone fragments, soon identified by a forensic anthropologist as belonging to a human female, and a false tooth were then found within a smokestack and in the drain pipe leading from the vat.

The police theorized that Luetgert had strangled his wife, dissolved her body in the acid vat (it was established that he had curiously ordered several pounds of caustic potash and arsenic on the day before her disappearance), and then burned the body remnants in a furnace.

As word of all this got out to the general public, sausage sales in the neighborhood inexplicably plummeted. Go figure.

Luetgert was arrested and charged with murder. During the trial, the prosecution actually obtained a corpse and boiled it in caustic potash (in Luetgert's very own vat) for two hours. The results (ugh!) closely matched the noxious residue the police had discovered during their investigation.

Adolph Luetgert was convicted of murder in February, 1898, and sent away to Joliet Penitentiary. It's been said that he became convinced his dead wife was haunting him and complained incessantly to his jailers. A tormented man right to the end, he died in 1900.

Over the years, there have been reports of Louisa Luetgert's ghost being seen, both in the factory building and surrounding neighborhood. One report was credible enough to once again draw police captain Schuettler, original investigating office in the murder almost four years before, back into the Luetgert saga. In April of 1901, Schuettler sent two of his police detectives to the factory, where flickering lights had been seen within the abandoned building. The detectives, accompanied by a night watchman, pursued a mysterious ball of light throughout the rooms, and at last down to the basement, where they claimed it came to rest at the very spot where the notorious boiling vat had once stood. And then it vanished.

If you visit the site, keep an eye out for a diminutive (Louisa stood less than 5' tall) blonde. She is said to appear in the area most often near May 1, the date of her untimely and grisly murder.

Today, the location has undergone many changes. In addition to the factory's conversion to condos, a second, smaller factory once there has vanished. In addition, the Luetgert home, which stood just behind the factory building, was moved—and its present location is somewhat of a mystery.

There is some evidence that it used to stand on Diversey Parkway, just west of Paulina Avenue, but it's now long gone, replaced by rows of townhomes. The house was said to have undergone significant renovations over the years. In 1907, a newspaper claimed, "A new coat of paint and a thorough renovation is believed to have so changed it that not even the ghost of Mrs. Luetgert, which was once said to haunt it, will know it again."

No matter. Once again, the townhomes win.

❀ *Bonus*: *Adolph Luetgert's Tavern: More Sausage.* 2201

N. Clybourn Avenue, Chicago IL 60614. Adolph Luetgert at one time before opening his sausage-making factory, owned a tavern at this location. There is some evidence that an enraged Luetgert killed a patron outside in a bizarre fashion, by shoving a wad of chewing tobacco down Hugh McGowan's throat until he choked. Reportedly, McGowan had refused Luetgert's warning to stop spitting tobacco juice on the sidewalk in front of the tavern. Luetgert, however, was never charged in the matter.

℘*Note:* Over the years, a lot of ghostly phenomena has been reported here. The building has long been rumored to have hosted nefarious activities over the years, including a child prostitution ring. As of September 2019, it was still a tavern.

The Fuchs Family Murders
1425 N. Hoffman Avenue, Park Ridge IL 60068
Park Ridge is a rather quiet, moderately-affluent suburb adjoining northwest Chicago. Nothing noteworthy ever seems to happen there. On the night of June 14, 1974, that would change. As the dinner hour approached on that Friday evening, 14-year-old Lynda Fuchs, visiting at a girlfriend's home, received a phone call. On the line was her 18-year-old brother, Jeff, who instructed her to return home. Lynda refused; she had previously received permission from their mother to spend time with her friend.

Later that evening, Lynda, accompanied by her friend, walked home. Saying goodbye, she entered the house and was never seen alive again.

Unbeknownst to Lynda, brother Jeff was patiently waiting for her inside—with homicidal intentions. The three other members of the Fuchs' family were already dead in the house. The body of their mother, Ruth, strangled and stabbed, lay on the basement floor, beside the bodies of their father, Raymond, and 16-year-old brother, Scott. The elder Fuchs had been shot in the head. Scott had been bludgeoned and strangled.

Jeff Fuchs shot Lynda in the head and lay her body beside the others. He then arranged an arson device, consisting of flammable liquids, rags, and two candles, in the basement. He lit the candles, apparently to conceal the nature of his crime by burning the house—and the evidence—to cinders. He then went upstairs to the kitchen. Seated at the kitchen table, he ingested a deadly cocktail of sleeping pills, aspirin and alcohol, and began an eternal sleep.

Jeff Fuchs's arson attempt did not go as planned. Instead of the house breaking into an inferno, the inside area simply smoldered—not even enough to alert neighbors. It wasn't until three days later that Mrs. Fuchs's grandmother, anxious by her inability to reach her daughter, entered the home and discovered the horror within.

What led a suburban kid like Jeffrey Fuchs to slaughter his entire family? No one will ever really know; the answer died with him. In the aftermath of the tragedy, that familiar description was heard from teachers and neighbors alike: "He was such a quiet kid."

While You are in Park Ridge:

A Burglary Turned to Tragedy:
The Lonesome Death Of Doug Moderow
43 S. Prospect Avenue, Park Ridge IL 60068

This site is now occupied by "Holt's," a casual restaurant, but for many years it was the home of Pine's Store for Men and Boys, which finally closed in 2013.

The tragic event that transpired here, way back in 1967 is of a highly personal nature to me. A high school friend committed suicide at Pine's during an amateurish burglary attempt. Of course, this was a major event in my youth.

But, time certainly does pass by quickly. My initial attempts to research the precise details of the story (to verify what I remembered) were incredibly unsuccessful. Even though the event was etched vividly into my memory, for the rest of the world it seemed completely forgotten. Even though 1967 does not seem *that* long ago, all accounts seemed to have vanished.

Doug Moderow and I attended Lane Tech from 1963 to graduation in January of 1967. Back in those days, they actually had both January and June graduations. Doug was an extremely intelligent kid, and he had a burning passion to make the world aware of it. He was always a natural rebel. I've always thought that he was mostly rebelling against his dad, who was a highly-respected school principal. He was forever talking about elaborate scams he would one day enact to demonstrate to the world just how smart he was. After leaving Lane, we drifted a bit away from each other. He lived in Park Ridge, and I lived in Chicago.

I hadn't spoken with him in months when I received word of his death.

With all that said, here's the basic story:

On the late afternoon of Wednesday, March 1, 1967, Doug equipped himself with tools and a revolver, concealed himself within a large television box, and had a friend transport the box, seated upon a Radio Flyer wagon, to Pine's. The friend then informed store authorities that he had a sudden family emergency to attend to, and asked permission to leave the box there in the store until returning for it the next day. Permission was granted.

After the store had closed for the night, Doug emerged from the box and began helping himself to the merchandise. While so engaged, he inadvertently tripped a burglar alarm, and police cars were soon pulling up in front of the store.

Before the police forcibly entered the premises, Doug placed the gun to his head and pulled the trigger. Why such an extreme action? Personally, I believe he was adamant about not having to face the further embarrassment his actions would cause his father. He had already been in and out of trouble many times. Can't prove it, but that's what I think.

Note: Researching this one was really tough. I found records of the incident hard to come by. I had my memories, but little else. Even the local police department couldn't help;

their records did not go back that far. Luckily, the kind folks at the Park Ridge Public Library came to the rescue, locating old newspaper articles buried in their archives.

Murder in Woodstock: No Peace and Love
209 W. Greenwood Avenue, Woodstock IL 60098

When you hear the word "Woodstock," what images come to mind? Gentle hippies with flowers in their hair, groovin' peacefully, right? Well, not in Woodstock, Illinois, in the early morning hours of August of 21, 1988.

Rick Church, then 19, had recently received two emotional blows. Upon returning from Northern Illinois University for the summer, he learned that his parents were separating. Possibly even more devastating news was that his girlfriend, Colleen Ritter, 17, had decided to break up with him. The fact that Church's stay at college had made their relationship a long-distance one was a factor, but more troubling for Colleen was his ever-growing possessiveness. Rick Church believed her parents had pushed her to dump him.

Church spent the night of August 21 at home, drinking and brooding. Early the next morning, he traveled through the still-dark streets to the Ritter home. He located a spare key and took a hammer from a toolshed on the property. Entering the house just after 5 AM, he made his way to the first- floor master bedroom. Raymond and Ruth Ann Ritter, Colleen's parents, were asleep. Raising the hammer again and again, Church bludgeoned the couple to death. He then made his way to an upstairs bedroom where he attacked Colleen's brother, Michael, 10, with a knife. Colleen, hearing the commotion, ran to her brother's aid, and Church turned his attention to her, stabbing her repeatedly. She managed to play dead and Church left. Grabbing the phone, Colleen dialed 911, but was interrupted by the return of Church, who tore the phone from the wall. The terrified girl ran downstairs and out the door with Church in pursuit. Luckily at this point aroused neighbors intervened, but Church escaped before police arrived.

Returning to his home, he tossed a few items into a bag and took off in his mother's truck. He would remain at large for three years.

In November of 1991, a police officer in Salt Lake City was dining in a barbecue joint when he noticed that a worker strongly resembled the description of a man he'd seen on a flier back at police headquarters. He returned the next day to the diner, where the owner informed him the man was "Danny Lee Carson." The police soon visited "Carson," who readily admitted that he was really Rick Church. Why? His lawyer claimed that Church was simply tired of running.

Richard Church was tried and convicted of two counts of murder, two counts of attempted murder, and one count of home invasion. The conviction ensured life with no chance of parole, and Church remains incarcerated to this day.

The Brown's Chicken Massacre
168 W. Northwest Highway (Route 14), Palatine IL 60067

On the night of January 8, 1993, seven employees, including the two owners, of a Brown's Chicken restaurant located here were brutally murdered. The horrific crime went unsolved for nine long years before an informant's tip cracked the case and led authorities to the killers.

Late on that cold Friday night, employees' relatives were growing concerned. Their loved ones were long overdue. A few hours past the restaurant's normal closing time, the parents of 16-year-old Michael Castro phoned the Palatine police department to voice their concerns; Guadaloupe Maldonado's wife also called in to report her husband had not returned home.

When officers arrived in the parking lot behind the darkened building at approximately 2:30 AM, they found the employees' entrance door unlocked. Once inside, they located the bodies of seven victims within a walk-in refrigerator. Some lay face-up, others face-down. They had all been shot, some also stabbed and slashed. Just under $2,000 had been removed from the cash register.

An intense investigation of the crime began immediately, but all leads soon became dead-ends. Authorities could only hope for an eventual break in the case.

The break finally came nine years later, in March 2002. A woman named Anne Lockett came forward with a claim that she had known the killers' identity from the start, but had remained quiet in fear for her life. She fingered a former boyfriend, James Degorski, and his friend, Juan Luna, as the perpetrators. She told police that Degorski had phoned her the night of the murders and told her to watch the news, because he "had done something big."[11]

Her claim would later be backed up by another Degorski friend, Eileen Bakalla, who reported that she had driven Degorski and Bakalla home in the early morning hours of January 9. Degorski had admitted his role in the slayings and instructed her to drive past the restaurant, where they could see groups of squad cars in the parking lot. Bakalla, like Lockett, indicated she had kept quiet in fear of her life.

James Degorski and Juan Luna were soon picked up and interrogated; both would be charged with murder.

A DNA analysis matched Luna's saliva to a piece of half-eaten chicken found at the restaurant, linking them to the crime. During subsequent court proceedings, it was learned that the pair had decided to perpetrate a major robbery. They chose Brown's because Luna had once worked there and knew the restaurant's routines. At some point, the robbery had gotten out of hand, and the shooting started.

Degorski and Luna would be found guilty of seven counts of murder and receive life sentences.

🔑*Note:* The Brown's Chicken location has been razed; a Chase Bank now stands at the site. Even so, there are more than a few Palatine residents who refuse to enter the building.

The Murderous Rampage of Laurie Dann
Hubbard Woods Elementary School, 110 Chatfield Road,
Winnetka IL 60093

In 1988, a highly-disturbed 30-year-old woman named Laurie (Wasserman) Dann embarked on a homicidal journey through the North Shore, resulting in the death of a young child and the wounding of many more. The community was left reeling from a shock it has not fully recovered from to this day. To add to locals' grief and outrage is the continuing conviction by many that Dann's parents did nothing to prevent the tragedy.

Born to an affluent family, Laurie Wasserman grew up in the northern Chicago suburb of Glencoe. A shy and withdrawn girl, her teenager years proved difficult. Even at an early age, she was displaying odd behaviors and compulsions. Her parents paid for plastic surgery in an effort to help her overcome her severe insecurities.

After graduation from New Trier High School, Laurie attended Drake University in Iowa, followed by a stint at the University of Arizona, but did not obtain a degree. When a romantic relationship with a pre-med student failed, she returned home. While working as a waitress, she met a successful executive in a family insurance business named Russell Dann and started a new relationship.

Russell and Laurie married in September 1982, and settled into a luxurious Highland Park home. Laurie Dann now appeared, at least outwardly, to have achieved her life's dream, but her odd behaviors, now bordering on the downright bizarre, would bring the marriage to an end.

She watched TV all day, refused to make the slightest attempt to keep the home clean, and would even inexplicably stuff dripping wet clothing into drawers. She also was becoming a virtual recluse, rarely leaving the house. Russell Dann tried hard to make the marriage work, but it was not destined to last.

In 1986, Russell was attacked with an ice pick while sleeping (which nearly killed him), but Laurie was never charged.

The couple divorced early in 1987, and Laurie moved back into her parents' home. She enrolled in many college classes, but failed to complete any. Her behavior now grew even more troubling. Her compulsive traits were by now on full display, including constant hand-washing and a disregard for personal hygiene.

Soon they were no longer confined to the home; she was displaying strange behavior everywhere. In addition, Russell

Dann and his relatives were now receiving anonymous threatening phone calls at all hours of the day and night. Dann now was accusing Russell of raping her. But Laurie's parents now were fully engaged in damage control, bailing her out of trouble and making excuses for her increasingly bizarre behaviors.

Laurie now began a babysitting business, but her clients soon began complaining about still more troubling behavior. They would often find their furniture slashed, money taken, and even raw meat tucked under sofa cushions. Still, the Wassermans continued to cover for her, paying restitutions, and allowing her to avoid consequences.

In January of 1988, Laurie Dann would enroll in classes at the University of Wisconsin in Madison—but, as usual, would complete none. While there, she saw a psychiatrist who adjusted her medications for obsessive compulsiveness and treated her for mood swings. But, her behaviors at the university continued to be troubling.

In fact, according to fellow dorm residents, her main activity was riding the elevators all day and night, pressing buttons randomly. She was also leaving rotting meat in the common areas, and would appear naked in the halls. Laurie was continuing to make threatening phone calls from her dorm room. When she was charged with shoplifting, her parents bailed her out yet again. On May 14, she was discovered naked and asleep on a garbage pile in the dorm.

She returned to Glencoe and attempted to restart her babysitting business. By this point, she had purchased three revolvers, which would soon be put to use. By March, she had stopped attending sessions with a psychiatrist, who had strongly recommended that Laurie be hospitalized. Laurie—and her enabling parents—refused to heed the suggestion.

In the early days of May 1988, Laurie Dann began the preparations for her final breakdown: she laced snacks with arsenic and loaded her pistols. On the morning of May 20, she dropped off her poisoned treats at several acquaintances' homes, Leverow Hall at Northwestern University, and homes of former babysitting clients. They were luckily poorly prepared; no one died. She picked up the children of an unsuspecting former client with the stated goal of taking them to a local carnival in Evanston. Instead, she drove to Ravinia Elementary School in Highland Park. Here, she attempted to detonate a homemade bomb, but it failed to explode.

Next, she drove to a nearby daycare center, which she believed another of her ex-sister-in-law's children was enrolled. Her attempt to enter the building with a can of gasoline was thwarted by the school security staff.

Laurie Dann then drove the children back to their Winnetka home (while trying to persuade them to drink tainted milk, which they refused). After dropping the children off, she attempted to set the home on fire. It was soon extinguished, and no one was hurt.

She then traveled three and a half blocks to the Hubbard Woods Elementary School. Gaining entry, she encountered a boy in the hall. She pushed him into a washroom and shot him with her .22 Beretta pistol. She then switched to her .357 Magnum handgun and fired at two other boys, but the gun jammed and she tossed it aside. Dann then entered a second grade classroom, where a heroic substitute teacher first unsuccessfully tried to engage her in a class activity and then bravely tried to thwart her when she saw she was brandishing a weapon. Dann managed to shoot five children, tragically killing one, an eight-year-old boy. She then left the building and fled in her car.

Nearby streets were flooded with traffic from a funeral cortege. Dann's escape route was hopelessly blocked. Abandoning her car, she set off on foot. She entered the nearby home of the Andrew family, where she announced that she had been raped, but had managed to kill her attacker. The Andrews managed to secure the Beretta handgun, but Laurie retained the .32. Mrs. Dann was called, and a protracted conservation between mother and daughter ensued. Unnoticed, Mrs. Andrew slipped out of the house and called authorities from a neighbor's phone.

Soon, police cars were pulling up in front of the residence. Dann, realizing that she had been duped by the Andrews, shot their son, Phillip, in the chest with her .32. He managed to escape with his life, staggering out of the house into the arms of the police.

Laurie Dann then went to an upstairs bedroom, where she took her life with a bullet in the mouth.

Laurie's parents have since passed on, but the bitterness of the community remains. Many believe that countless warning signs were ignored by the Wasserman family, ultimately leading to a needless tragedy.

Laurie Dann's Suicide Site. 2 Kent Road, Winnetka IL 60093. Laurie Dann shot young Phillip Andrew here before heading to an upstairs bedroom to take her own life.

Laurie Wasserman Dann Grave Shalom Memorial Park, 1700 W. Rand Road, Arlington Heights IL 60004.

5. GLITZ & GLAMOUR CHICAGO

Essanay Studios
1345 W. Argyle Street, Chicago IL 60640

Before there was MGM, Paramount, United Artists and Warner Brothers—hell, before there was Hollywood—there was the iconic Essanay Studios. George Spoor and Gilbert An-

The Essanay Studios on Argyle Street: Chicago's very own version of Hollywood.

derson founded the Peerless Film Manufacturing Company in 1907, but the name was quickly changed to Essanay, reflecting the owners' initials "S" and "A."

The studio produced films starring Ben Turpin, Gloria Swanson, Wallace Beery, Francis X. Bushman, Broncho Billy Anderson, Colleen Moore, and their biggest star, Charlie Chaplin. (Chaplin would only stay in Chicago for one year before heading to California.) Chaplin's classic film, *The Tramp*, was shot right here.

Chicago's variable weather patterns eventually dictated a move to more film-friendly locations out west, and Essanay Studios soon went into decline.

But it was Hollywood before there was Hollywood.

The main building still stands here on Argyle, with the chiseled "Essanay" logo still proudly visible over the door.

Charlie Chaplin's Chicago Apartment
2899 N. Pine Grove Avenue, Chicago IL 60657
(the penthouse)

Chaplin, one of the first true film megastars, lived here in the penthouse apartment in 1915 while filming at the Essanay Studios. He was being paid $1,250 per week—absolutely enormous money in 1915.

Note: The apartment building is still here.

Gloria Swanson
"All right, Mr. DeMille. I'm ready for my close-up."
3710 N. Kenmore Avenue, Chicago IL 60613

Gloria Swanson started out as a silent movie star at the nearby Essanay Studios, but her films there are all but forgotten; what she is really known for was her spectacularly creepy depiction of the faded, delusional—and very weird—movie queen Norma Desmond in the 1950 classic, *Sunset Boulevard*.

Her family was living in this home near Wrigley Field in 1914, the year the teenage Gloria began appearing in films for Essanay Studios.

Swanson would go on to have a long film career—and somewhat scandalous life. She had one of the shortest marriages in Hollywood history (before it became fashionable), leaving actor Wallace Beery, whom she had married on her 17th birthday, shortly after tying the knot. She would later be widely rumored to be the paramour of Kennedy family patriarch Joe (father of JFK and RFK).

After a long period of career-decline, she re-emerged to deliver a truly knockout performance in Billy Wilder's *Sunset Boulevard*—perhaps the fabled "role-she-was-born-to-play."

Note: The house is still here.

The Rainbo Gardens
Where Moe and Shemp met Larry
4812-4836 N. Clark Street, Chicago IL 60640

This was the site of the Rainbo Gardens, a very popular entertainment hot spot during the Roaring Twenties. It offered a mix of traditional vaudeville acts, hot jazz and featured easy dance and liquor opportunities.

In 1925, Moe and Shemp Howard, seeking to break away from comedian Ted Healy's act—and form a comedy group of their own—first met Larry Fine here, and were impressed with him. (He was working as a master of ceremonies.) The Three Stooges were soon born.

Note: The building is long gone.

The Real Wizard of Oz: L. Frank Baum
1667 N. Humboldt Boulevard, Chicago IL 60647

The man who wrote *The Wonderful Wizard of Oz* composed

it here. He was living in a home at this site in 1900 when the book was first published, and it's certain he wrote much of it here. It's said that Baum was tremendously influenced by the Chicago World's Fair of 1893, and the sights served as inspiration for his Emerald City. A military academy in New York, which he had attended, had a road made of yellow brick; thus the yellow brick road was born.

The neatest part: Baum claimed that as he pondered a name for the magical land he had created, his eyes came to rest on a file cabinet, with a drawer labeled O-Z.

Just how cool is that?

Note: For many years, only a small plaque identified this spot. However, Chicago city fathers have recently realized its literary significance and have constructed an actual yellow brick road in front of the property.

Walt Disney's Boyhood Home
2156 N. Tripp Avenue, Chicago IL 60639

Walt Disney, one of America's greatest entertainment giants, was born in a house here in 1901. The family would move away to Missouri for a spell in 1906 but would return to the area by 1917. Walt would attend McKinley High School and later, The Art Institute. He would eventually leave Chicago for California, where he achieved cinematic immortality.

Mickey Mouse was (kind of) born in Chicago!

Note: The home is still here.

Hugh Hefner

The Playboy Mansion: Hugh Hefner's Pleasure Palace
1340 N. State Parkway, Chicago IL 60610
A sign above the door of this Gold Coast mansion read, "Si Non Oscillas, Noli Tintinnare." (If You Don't Swing, Don't

Ring.)[12] This was the notorious home base of Chicago's Playboy empire tycoon Hugh Hefner. One can only imagine the debauchery that took place inside this place.

Note: Hef had a 100"-diameter bed upstairs with "more controls and more gadgets than a Boeing 707."

Hugh Hefner's Boyhood Home
1922 N. New England Avenue, Chicago IL 60707
Before he was "Hef," he was just another Northwest-side kid, living here with his family. He published a typewritten newspaper, which he sold for a penny each in the neighborhood.

Commissioner Gordon's Porch: Batman In Chicago
4656 N. Clifton Avenue, Chicago IL 60640

There are many locations in Chicago where scenes for the Christian Bale *Batman* movies were filmed. Tour buses will often point out streets and buildings throughout the Loop where action scenes took place. Pretty impersonal stuff. I prefer this little-known spot in Uptown.

Now, I admit this one is strictly based on hearsay. Can't prove the veracity. *But*, the engineers at a recording studio here swear the courtyard was used for a Batman scene.

Do you remember the scene in *Batman Begins* where Batman (Christian Bale) chats with Commissioner Gordon (Gary Oldman) on Gordon's back porch? Well, reportedly it was filmed in the courtyard just behind this building. If you are feeling intrepid, wind your way around to the back and pop in for a look.

Note: Caution advised. This area of N. Clifton is a bit dicey. In fact, it's known to some as "Blood Alley."

Steve Allen:
A Poor Kid From Hyde Park

Talk show host, comedian and composer Steve Allen (1921-2000) was a familiar and beloved television personality for over 50 years. He is best remembered for being the original host of The Tonight Show, one of the first truly successful late-night talk shows. Allen hosted the show from 1954-57 and originated many of the talkshow staples still in use today: an opening monologue, celebrity interviews, and outrageous comedy bits (often conducted in the street outside the studio).

Allen was also an accomplished musician and songwriter, and was the composer of a huge hit still popular today: *This Could Be the Start of Something (Big).*

Steve Allen's Boyhood Home
5309 S. Kimbark Avenue, Chicago IL 60615

Allen's parents were vaudeville performers. He was still an infant when his father died, leaving the family in dire economic straits. His mother decided the best way to make ends meet was to carry on her show business career. Allen was left in the care of Chicago relatives. He spent the bulk of his youth in the Hyde Park neighborhood centered around 55th Street and Kimbark Avenue.

The Depression years were tough times for almost everyone, and Allen's guardian family was forced to move from larger apartments to smaller, less expensive ones. Most of the buildings are now gone, but this one remains.

Steve Allen hated this apartment, mainly because of the vermin problem. He would later write about his youth in a book, *But Seriously: Steve Allen Speaks His Mind.*

"I know what it's like to live with rats too, man. In my one room at 5309 Kimbark Avenue on the south side of Chicago they were so determined that we couldn't keep them from paying us daily visits." [13]

Hopefully, the rat problem on Kimbark Avenue has finally been taken care of.

Kim Novak
1910 S. Springfield Avenue, Chicago IL 60623

Kim Novak is one of the icy, cool blonde heroines so prized by director Alfred Hitchcock in the 1950s (others were Grace Kelly, Eva Marie Saint, Tippi Hedron and Janet Leigh).

She grew up at this address, attending Farragut High School and Wright Junior College. While on a trip to Los Angeles, she attracted the attention of Columbia Pictures, who signed her to a contract. Novak had strong opinions, even as a Hollywood newcomer, and wanted to carve an identity as an original film presence.

To this end, she battled with Columbia studio chief Harry Cohn over changing her name. Cohn wanted to change it to "Kit Marlowe," supposedly declaring, "Nobody's gonna go see a girl with a Polack name,"[14] but Novak held firm and won.

She would star in such films as *Picnic, Jeanne Eagels, Pal Joey, Vertigo* and *Bell, Book and Candle.*

Novak largely withdrew from Hollywood in 1966, and has only acted sporadically since.

Clayton Moore:
The Lone Ranger in Chicago
6254 N. Glenwood Avenue, Chicago IL 60660

The Lone Ranger himself, Clayton Moore, was born here in 1914. The future star of the 1950s television western hit attended nearby Hayt Elementary School and Senn High School. Moore would often claim that he first encountered, and immediately loved, western films at Saturday matinees at the Granada Theater, near Sheridan and Devon (now gone).

Moore was an excellent athlete and performed with an acrobatic troupe, known as The Flying Behrs, at the 1933 Century of Progress World's Fair held on the lake front. He moved to New York at age 19 to work as a John Roberts Powell model.

By 1938, he was in Hollywood, where he began appearing in small roles in western serials. In 1949, he won the role of *The Lone Ranger* in the hit TV show, which ran until 1957. Virtually every child who grew up in 1950s America would forever recognize Rossini's *William Tell Overture* as *The Lone Ranger Theme.*

Moore would continue to make personal appearances as The Lone Ranger, along with costar (and "Kemo Sabe") Jay Silverheels, for decades after the series ended. Throughout his life, he strived to maintain the sterling reputation his character represented as a role model for children. He passed away in 1999.

Note: Moore never forgot his Chicago roots. In 1985, he showed up at the doorstep of his old Glenwood Avenue home, and asked the current owners if he could have a look around. They gladly complied with his request.

Note: His Hollywood Walk of Fame plaque is the only one that lists both his name and the character he portrayed. It reads, "Clayton Moore—The Lone Ranger."

Hi-Yo, Silver. Away!

The Marx Brothers
4512 S. King Drive (S. Grand Boulevard in 1914)
Chicago IL 60653

"Groucho" (Julius), "Chico" (Leonard), "Harpo: (Adolph), "Gummo" (Milton) and "Zeppo" (Herbert) were, of course, the members (and brothers) of the legendary comedy group, The Marx Brothers. And although they were born in New York, they lived here in Chicago (or at least maintained a residential base here) from about 1910 until 1926.

As members of an ever-touring vaudeville act following a national circuit, the Marx Brothers decided that a headquarters in the Midwest would make sense. Since the Windy City was the main American railroad hub, linking all major cities, they settled here, first at an apartment at 4649 Calumet Avenue before purchasing this stone three-flat apartment building on (then) S. Grand Boulevard (now S. King Drive).

When the United States entered World War I, the Marx family had an alternative home on a LaGrange area farm. It was believed by many that farmers would be exempt from a military draft.

Once their careers took off due to great successes on Broadway, the Marx Brothers moved back to New York permanently in 1920. They eventually sold the house in 1926.

Note: The home is still here.

Benny Goodman
1125 S. Francisco Avenue, Chicago IL 60612

Benny Goodman (born 1909), "The King of Swing," was a wildly successful big bandleader and clarinetist during the 1930s and 40s.

The son of Russian immigrants, he shared this home, located in what then was a Jewish neighborhood, with 11 siblings. It was here that he would practice the clarinet after returning from music lessons at a local synagogue. Goodman would eventually join a band at the nearby Jane Adam's Hull House settlement where his talent blossomed. He would soon move to New York, where he joined a series of bands before organizing one of his own. Goodman's band caught fire with the public, and he was widely credited with creating "The Era of Swing," a style of music springing from jazz and instantly popular with audiences.

Note: The apartment building is still here, but the neighborhood has deteriorated over the years. Goodman, at age 76, returned for a visit in 1985, but reportedly never left his cab.

Michael Gross:
Northwest Side Family
Ties & Tremors

Actor Michael Gross, unlike the vast majority of performers today, can actually convincingly portray characters who are temperamental and emotional opposites.

For example, he was a most believable, laidback, ex-hippie dad, Steven Keaton, on the TV sitcom *Family Ties*, and later was able to effortlessly make the transition to a completely differently-wired character: Burt Gummer, the gun-loving ultra-survivalist star of the *Tremors* film franchise.

The Gross family lived in this modest home here on the Northwest side. Michael attended nearby St. Genevieve Grammar School and Kelvyn Park High School, where he was voted senior class president.

Michael Gross Boyhood Home. 2255 N. Kilbourn Avenue, Chicago IL 60639. The home is still here.

Dennis Farina
549 W. North Avenue, Chicago IL 60610

Chicago cop-turned-actor Dennis Farina was a true Windy City success story. Born in 1944, he was the youngest of seven children and grew up in a house that once stood here, on the western fringe of Old Town. Farina's career path sounds a bit like something straight out of a movie script.

After completing high school, he joined the Army for a three-year stint. Upon discharge, he returned home, soon joining the Chicago police force, where he served for 18 years.

As a sidelight during this time, he began moonlighting as an actor.

His big break, which allowed him to transition to a full-time acting career, came in 1986 with a role on the television series *Crime Story*, which ran through 1988. Prominent roles in films soon followed: *Midnight Run* (with Robert DeNiro), *Manhunter, Saving Private Ryan* and *Get Shorty*. Another hit television series role (as Detective Joe Fontana) in *Law & Order* (2004-2006) further cemented his screen status as a tough, blunt-talking "Chicago guy."

Farina never forgot his roots, often visiting old Chicago haunts to spend time with his old neighborhood friends, as well as former police force buddies. He passed away in 2013 from complications of lung cancer.

Note: The North Avenue home is gone, replaced by townhomes.

Opinion: We have all been subjected over the years to actors futilely attempting to sound like genuine ChiGAHgo tough guys. Farino nailed it.

Bob Fosse
4428 N. Paulina Street, Chicago IL 60640

Celebrated dance/choreographer Bob Fosse (1927-1987) grew up in this two-story red brick home in Ravenswood. At age nine, he began accompanying an older sister to dance lessons at the Chicago Academy of Dance & Theatre, which stood at Ashland and Montrose. Although his original focus was on a girl there, he quickly displayed a natural gift for dance and began to practice relentlessly. He would soon partner with another neighborhood lad, and they began performing together locally as an act called The Riff Brothers.

Following a stint in the Navy, Fosse married and began performing as a dancer in New York, along with his first wife, Mary Ann. Comedian Jerry Lewis caught their act at a club there, was impressed and recommended him to show business associates.

He was soon signed to an MGM contract. Fosse now began a long string of successes as a choreographer. His creative work on the film *Kiss Me Kate* brought him to the attention of

Broadway stage producers, and he quickly became regarded as the hottest choreographer in New York.

Along the way, he would marry his fourth and final wife, dancer/actress Gwen Verdon (where did he find all that time?). The hits *The Pajama Game, Damn Yankees, New Girl in Town, Redhead, How to Succeed in Business Without Really Trying, Sweet Charity* and *Pippin* continued to cement his lofty reputation. Perhaps his greatest projects, and the ones he is best known for, were *Chicago* and *All That Jazz*, both successfully transitioned for films.

Note: The house still stands.

Jack Johnson in the House
Graceland Cemetery, 4001 N. Clark Street, Chicago IL 60613
Bellevue Section, Lot 437, Space 1

Jack Johnson, a legendary boxer, was the first black American Heavyweight Champion, holding the title from 1908 – 1915. His boxing successes, compounded by his marriage to a white woman (Etta) infuriated many whites in a country still dominated by anti-black sentiments. He would even be targeted by law enforcement authorities with a host of somewhat dubious charges. He would eventually leave the US to avoid the persecution.

As soon as Johnson secured his boxing title, a search was on for a "Great White Hope"; a white fighter who could retake the crown from him. This finally happened on April 5, 1915, when Jess Willard knocked Johnson out (26th round) in a fight held in Havana, Cuba.

Johnson, after losing his title, found his prospects in decline. He would continue to fight (until age 60!) to keep financially afloat, although his ring skills were quickly eroding. Johnson died in a North Carolina car crash in 1946.

Note: Muhammad Ali was a great admirer of Jack Johnson. During fights, in an effort to energize and inspire Ali, his flamboyant corner man Bundini Brown would shout, "Jack Johnson in the house!" [15]

Johnson is buried at the foot of wife Etta's grave.

6. GLITZ & GLAMOUR
SUBURBS AND BEYOND

Lots of celebs seem to have a very real connection to the northern suburbs of Chicago. Some, such as Charlton Heston, Ann-Margret and Bill Murray, lived here as kids. Others, such as Harold Ramis, John Hughes and Michael Jordan, chose to build their luxurious estates here later in life. Who needs Beverly Hills?

Charlton Heston:
Moses on the North Shore

Charlton Heston was the quintessential Hollywood movie star, appearing in such classics as *The Ten Commandments, Ben-Hur, Touch of Evil, El Cid, Planet of the Apes* and so many more. With his commanding appearance and sonorous voice, his was a commanding screen presence. But, he spent a lot of his boyhood here.

Heston was born in 1923 on the North Shore, most likely in Evanston (it's a bit murky). While still an infant, the family moved to Michigan. Later, his parents divorced and his mother and new husband brought the family back to this area, settling into a modest home in Wilmette. This is where most of his boyhood was spent. Heston would later attend New Trier High School.

After attaining stardom in Hollywood, he would comment, "We lived in a North Shore suburb, where I was a skinny hick from the woods, and all the other kids seemed to be rich and know about girls." [16]

Charlton Heston's Boyhood Home
325 Maple Avenue, Wilmette IL 60091

Note: The home is still here.

Ann-Margret: Wilmette Firecracker

Ann-Margret, the sultry, singin', swivelin' Swedish silver screen spitfire was once just plain old Ann-Margret Olsson, daughter of Anna and Gus.

The family arrived in the US when she was only five and spoke no English. They settled in Wilmette in 1948. Apparently, Ann-Margret was a quick learner. Once enrolled at New Trier High School, her prodigious talents soon began to blossom. She even caused a controversy in her senior year by performing a "too steamy" rendition (according to some parents) of the song *Tropical Heat Wave* in a school show. Hollywood would soon beckon.

But, while here in Wilmette, the Olsson's lived quite modestly. Records indicate that the family resided in at least 2 different locations :

Ann-Margret lived here #1
1315 Wilmette Avenue, Wilmette IL 60091
This modest home, located on the south side of Wilmette Avenue, dates back to 1880. This was most likely the first Olsson family residence in Wilmette.

Ann-Margret lived here #2
725 Ridge, Wilmette IL 60091
After father Gus was severely injured in a work accident, the family lived in a section of this building, then a funeral

home, where Anna worked as a receptionist. As of 2019, the funeral home is no more, reborn as a picture-framing business.

Right next to the location is a really atmospheric little neighborhood bowling alley. Dating back to 1927, the Wilmette Bowling Center appears an awful lot like just a local corner tavern.

Undoubtedly, young Ann-Margret would often fall asleep to the mixed sounds of mourners and rattling ten-pins.

Note: Both houses remain.

Rock Hudson: Roy Harold Scherer, Jr.?

Before there was Tab Hunter, before there was Troy Donahue, there was Rock Hudson.

The prototypical Hollywood-studio-created beefsteak/ pretty boy actor of the 50s and 60s, Hudson was first placed in action films, like *Gun Fury* (1953), *Son of Cochise* (1954), and *Bengal Brigade* (1954), and then allowed to try his hand at straight dramas, like *Giant*, with James Dean (1956), and *Something of Value,* with Sidney Poitier (1957).

Whatever he may have lacked in acting skills seemed to be more than made up for with terrific looks. Tall, dark & handsome, Hudson found his true niche in 1959 with light, frothy romantic comedy/"pillow-talk" films like … well, *Pillow Talk*, opposite Doris Day.

A string of similar vehicles followed: *Lover Come Back* (61), *Man's Favorite Sport* (64), *Send Me No Flowers* (64), and *Strange Bedfellows* (65).

Hudson's status as a hunky leading man began to dramatically decline soon after as his penchant for frequenting gay leather bars was becoming increasingly noticed and commented upon. By 1970, his co-star in *Darling Lili*, Julie Andrews, was reported by a gossip columnist as having to remind Hudson that she, not he, was the leading lady. The Hudson and Andrews pairing was referred to by *The Village Voice* as "the least convincing couple in screen history … Their supposedly steamy love scene had as much fizzle as day-old beer."[17]

Hudson was able to right the ship in 1971 by turning to television. *McMillan and Wife* (1971-1977) was a hit, as was a later series, *Dynasty*.

Despite a successful acting career, Rock Hudson is perhaps best known for being the first actor to publicly acknowledge he was suffering from AIDS in July of 1985. He would soon die of the disease, aged 59, in October of that same year.

Ah, but before there was Rock Hudson, there was Roy Harold Scherer, Jr. That was the name he went by growing up in Winnetka, at least until his parents divorced in 1935. He took his new stepfather's name and was now known as Roy Fitzgerald.

His family sure moved around a lot. Records indicate that the family lived at various times in at least six locations in the village.

Three are now long gone. Here are the three still there:

Rock Hudson lived here #1
1017 Elm Street, Winnetka IL 60093
A modest home (for Winnetka, which is pretty ritzy). Records indicate that the family lived here in 1929.

Rock Hudson lived here #2
809 Chestnut Court, Winnetka IL 60093
Now this small apartment building, right in the thick of the village, was very cool, from the faux-Tudor look to the winding staircase leading upstairs. The date "1927" is etched in stone on the front façade. Records indicate that the family was living here in 1935.

Rock Hudson lived here #3
907 Ash Street, Winnetka IL 60093
Another modest home, this one is noteworthy for being the probable family home at the time young Roy Fitzgerald began attending New Trier High School (1940).

Bruce Dern:
Born With a Silver Spoon

One of my favorite crazy bad guys of film. Not quite as maniacal as Jack Palance, perhaps, but still. It's hard to not like one of the very few guys to kill John Wayne with a shot in the back (*The Cowboys*, 1972).

Dern was born (1936) and raised to an old money family in Winnetka. His grandfather was a governor of Utah (later Secretary of War in the FDR administration). His great-uncle was renowned poet Archibald MacLeish, and his godfather was senator and later presidential candidate, Adlai Stevenson. Talk about blue blood!

Dern attended—surprise!—New Trier High School before heading west to make his mark in the movies.

Bruce Dern's Boyhood Home
94 Mary Street, Winnetka IL 60093
Truly, a castle-like mansion. I think Brucie deserves a lot of credit for the motivation to strike out on his own and pursue a career. Personally, in his position I would have been sorely tempted to simply sit in a big comfy armchair and listen to the sounds of my inheritances piling up.

New Trier High School:
The Petri Dish of North Shore Stars
385 Winnetka Avenue, Winnetka, IL 60093

Here are a few of the famous who attended: Actors Charlton Heston, Ann-Margret, Rock Hudson, Bruce Dern, Rainn Wilson (*The Office*), Hugh O'Brien (TV's *Wyatt Earp*); film director John Hughes; U.S. Secretary of Defense Donald Rumsfeld; musicians Liz Phair and Pete Wentz; and author Scott Turow.

Bill Murray: Caddy Extraordinaire

New Trier High School. Where the stars matriculated.

Bill Murray? You probably feel like you practically know the guy, after all those wonderful films: *Meatballs, Stripes, Caddyshack, Ghostbusters 1 & 2, Scrooged, Groundhog Day, Zombieland, Lost in Translation, St. Vincent...* And those are just a few.

You probably also know that Murray got his career started at Chicago's famed improv theater, The Second City, before hitting it big in Hollywood. Really, really big.

And you probably also know Bill's reputation as the true eccentric's eccentric. He is the unchallenged Major Hollywood Star champion of a noble and rare ambition: the quest to just be a regular guy. Bill still spends a lot of time in the area. He can often be seen cheering on his beloved Cubs at Wrigley Field, crashing the occasional wedding, and ferreting out random karaoke opportunities.

Bill's Boyhood Home
1930 Elmwood Avenue, Wilmette IL 60091
Bill was one of nine siblings growing up in this very modest

Wilmette's Mallinckrodt Park. A young Bill Murray and his brothers often played here.

Wilmette home. With such a large family (and so few bathrooms!) and constantly overstretched finances, the Murrays, by necessity, grew up a close-knit clan. It was said that dinnertimes often served as comedy vehicles for the kids to outperform each other. This atmosphere, no doubt, was of great later value to Bill.

While you are here, check out the park across the street (*Mallinckrodt Park*). With nine kids crammed into a small house facing it, I'm sure it received more than its share of Murray family hijinks.

The Indian Hill Club
(where Bill Murray learned all about golf)
1 N. Indian Hill Road, Winnetka IL 60093

Just up the road north of the Murray home is the Indian Hill Club. Here then, surely, was the genesis/birthplace for Carl Spackler, the hapless assistant groundskeeper character Murray created for the classic comedy, *Caddyshack*. Bill and his five brothers caddied here, and many of the characters and situations in the film (Bill's older brother, Brian, wrote much of the script) were based on the brothers' experiences here.

All five were inducted into the Caddy Hall of Fame in 2015. So they got that going for them. Which is nice.

I love Bill's advice for young caddies: "The mark of a good caddie is the ability to look at a player when he hits a bad shot and go 'eh … it happens.' And when he hits a good shot, you go, 'Well, that's really who you are.'"[18]

Groundhog Day Filming Sites
Woodstock IL 60098

Okay, this is a little bit of a trek from the Bill Murray Wilmette/Winnetka sites, but maybe after checking them out you are now in a real B.M. mood (snicker).

Set the old GPS for Woodstock, IL. It was here that most of the filming was done for 1992's *Groundhog Day*. You can step off the same curb Murray did when trying to avoid a pushy insurance salesman (now known as "Ned's Corner"). The slushy pothole/puddle's gone now, but it's still a cool thing to do.

You can also dine at the same joint where Bill shoved food into his face and drank coffee straight from the pot. (It was the Tip Top Café in the film. Now it's a Mexican restaurant.)

Visit the spot (the town square) where Punxsutawny Phil made his weather prediction.

Stroll the alley where Bill found the dying old man (Old Man's Alley), and drop in at the site of the "big dance," where the pivotal last scenes of the film took place (the Woodstock Moose Lodge).

While you are there, check out the Woodstock Opera House on the town square. It's said to be haunted by "Elvira," the ghost of a young actress who jumped to her death from the highest tower of the building in the early 1900s. Seat 113 seems to be her favorite.

Note: Orson Welles, the famed director/actor, attended a nearby boy's school (Todd School) in the area and performed at the Opera House on several occasions (more about him in a moment). Since you're already here, take a short trip northeast to visit the only remaining building from the Todd

School campus. After all, the guy who created *Citizen Kane*, often regarded as the greatest movie ever made, got his creative mojo going here.

Orson Welles: A Renaissance Man in Woodstock & Kenosha

Orson Welles was a flat-out genius. Not only did he create (and/or star in) such film gems as *Citizen Kane* (1941), *The Magnificent Ambersons* (1942), *The Third Man* (1949) and *Touch of Evil* (1958), he terrified the entire nation in 1938 with his Mercury Players' radio broadcast of *War of the Worlds*. And who can ever forget those sonorous, Shakespearean wine commercials?

And, oh, by the way, he was only 25 years old when he made *Citizen Kane!*

Rogers Hall (Todd School for Boys):
Where Orson Welles Blossomed
730 N. Seminary Avenue, Woodstock IL 60098

Rogers Hall, where a young Orson Welles came into his own.

This is the last remaining building from the campus of the Todd School For Boys (opened in 1848). It was here, in 1926, that 11-year-old Orson Welles received the eclectic education that unlocked the creative juices that would manifest in the years ahead. Late in life, when Welles was asked what he considered his "home," he identified Woodstock and Todd School.

One particular teacher (later headmaster), Roger Hill, encouraged Welles' passion here for all things theatrical, allowing him to blossom creatively. "I was passionate about the theatre—putting on plays was all I ever wanted to do with my life—and Skipper, God bless him, was the only one of my elders who encouraged my theatrical ambitions."[19]

Hill would remain a lifelong friend and mentor.

Note: Woodstock, for some, might seem to lack a sense of historical nostalgia; every other Todd edifice has been razed over the years. Rogers Hall has been converted to an apartment building: Rogers Hall Apartments.

Up for a little ride?

Orson Welles' Boyhood Home
6116 7th Avenue, Kenosha WI 53140

Okay, this one requires you to do a bit of driving, but it's well worth it. Orson Welles lived here from the time of his birth until about age five.

He remained ambivalent about Kenosha for his entire life. At various times he said, "I have been to Kenosha in recent years and found it vital and charming." (1937). Years later, he said, "I'm not ashamed of being from Wisconsin. Just of being from Kenosha. It's a terrible place."[20]

It has been postulated that his negative feelings about his hometown had a lot to do with the death of his mother in 1924. His parents separated in 1919, and both relocated to Chicago, but she asked to be buried in Kenosha. She was buried there on "a bleak day" that haunted Welles for his entire life.

Somewhat surprisingly, Kenosha does not really celebrate this hometown son all that much—perhaps because of the negative comments Welles made about the town over the years. This modest home, now a duplex, does have a simple plaque, but you get the feeling that he deserves much, much more recognition.

Welles died in 1985, age 70, in Hollywood. His ashes were placed within a well (at a bullfighter's residence) in Spain. Of course. *But*, his parents were both interred in Kenosha. And you can pay your respects, as Orson did in 1924 and 1930.

Graves of Orson Welles' Parents: Green Ridge Cemetery
6604 7th Avenue, Kenosha WI 53143
Section Southeast: Block 52, Lot 1

☀ As Long As You're Out Here / On the Way Back:

You're a tad north of the Cheddar Curtain and you will be heading back south. How about visiting a few more sites connected to celebrated figures along the way?

Bob Collins
Midwestern Regional Medical Center
2610 Sheridan Road, Zion IL 60099

Bob Collins was a very popular radio personality on Chicago's very own WGN. Known affectionately as "Uncle Bobby," his show maintained top ratings from 1986 until his untimely death. And he loved flying, often talking about the joys of aviation on-air.

On the afternoon of February 8, 2000, Collins' small plane, soon after departing from Waukegan Regional Airport, collided with another craft flown by a young student pilot. Both planes crashed. The student pilot's Cessna landed in a street, killing her instantly. Collins' plane crashed onto the roof of this medical center. He, along with a passenger friend, died instantly.

✎ *Note:* I was a guest on his radio show once, discussing a rock & roll game I had created (Collins liked rock & roll). The game would go on to bomb spectacularly.

John Alexander Dowie
Shiloh House
1300 Shiloh Boulevard, Zion IL 60099

Just steps north of the Midwestern Medical Center stands the opulent home of one John Alexander Dowie, a religious leader who attempted to mold Zion into a religious utopia. Born in Scotland, Dowie was the founder of the Christian Catholic Church. In 1900, he established the city of Zion as a community where his followers would be free of the evils of modern society, a self-sustaining community where "God ruled."

Of course, human nature being what is, things eventually went bad. Dowie's extravagant spending habits, highlighted by the building of this mansion, began to trouble his flock. Eventually, Dowie was unseated from his leadership role. He was allowed to live out the remainder of his years here in Shiloh House until his death in 1907.

✎ *Note:* Shiloh House offers tours. The mansion is well worth visiting. The surrounding neighborhood is now a lot of open land, but it was once filled with the homes of Dowie's flock. A sizable number still remain.

Jack Benny
518 W. Clayton St., Waukegan IL 60085

Jack Benny was a wildly popular radio (and later movie and TV) star from the 30s through the 60s. Although born in Chicago (1894), he would grow up in Waukegan, which has never forgotten him. He would develop a vaudeville act here and often performed in the area.

In 1909, young Benny (then Benjamin Kubelsky) lived with his family in this modest two-story home. There is a plaque there identifying the site, and the Jack Benny Middle School is only a short walk away.

Abraham Lincoln in Waukegan

Abraham Lincoln's only documented visit to Lake County occurred in April 1860. He took a train from Chicago to Waukegan for dinner and an overnight stay at the home of a friend, Elisha P. Ferry. While there, a fire broke out in a nearby warehouse, and it's said that Mr. Lincoln rolled up his sleeves and helped extinguish the blaze.

The Ferry Home: Lincoln really did sleep here
308 Julian Street, Waukegan IL 60085

Note: The home is still standing, although it has undergone considerable restorations over the years.

Marlon Brando:
His Tango in Libertyville

Okay, you really should be headed back to the North Shore to continue the tour. But what if I told you that the Godfather himself, Marlon Friggin' *Brando*, once lived on a farm in Libertyville, not too far away from where you are now, from 1937 to 1941? He went to high school there (before getting yanked), began really cultivating that iconic bad boy image, and even ushered at a local movie theater (before getting fired)? You'd want to go, right?

Marlon Brando's Farm/Home
Bradley Road (south of Route 176/Rockland Road)
Libertyville IL 60044

Marlon Brando once lived on a farm in this now-overgrown area near Libertyville.

I admit the exact location of this one involves some guesswork. Here's what I know: Brando's immediate family was regarded as highly dysfunctional. Both parents were said to be alcoholics and always fighting. After a separation, they decided to give peace—and their family—a chance, and moved to a farm in Libertyville. The records indicate that they purchased (or leased) the land formerly owned by one "J.B. Wheeler" on Bradley Road.

Marlon, his two sisters, dad, and mom moved in. The family troubles didn't stop with the move to rural surroundings. Supposedly, Marlon's mom would get wasted in nearby taverns and often have to be dragged home by Dad. Dad would frequently beat mom (and sometimes, Marlon). You know, your typical family stuff.

Marlon eventually left for acting stardom. The family remained. He would often come back to visit. The land was eventually sold to make way for a housing development, and the home vanished.

Now then: Where exactly was the farmhouse?

I'm not sure. Once you arrive at the intersection of Bradley Road & 176, head south. You will be in the general area of the Brando farm. It's a pretty little area, lots of green dotted with a bit of light industry, storage facilities, and a couple of equestrian farms.

The Brando home would have been on the east side of the road, just about opposite from where the post office now stands (on the west side of the road).

Where Marlon Brando went to high school
Libertyville High School
708 W. Park Avenue, Libertyville IL 60048
He was viewed as an outsider here from the outset. Libertyville "townie" students regarded him as one living on the wrong side of the tracks. Besides that, he hadn't grown up in the area and didn't have friends. His volatile temperament probably didn't help.

Brando himself characterized his time at Libertyville High School thusly: "I was a bad student, chronic truant, and all-around incorrigible." [21]

Would you expect anything less? The Wild One? He was soon kicked out. Various reports cite poor grades, smoking, and skating (or biking) down the halls.

His dad sent him off to a military academy, where he was quickly kicked out. Surprise.

Where Marlon Brando worked as an usher
Liberty Theater, 708 N. Milwaukee Avenue,
Libertyville IL 60048
Marlon, known as "Bud" to family and friends, began working here in 1939. It's no big surprise that he quickly began to chafe under the policies involved in the job. He didn't like the uniform requirements, for starters, so he replaced the stiff dress shirt under his formal usher jacket with an undershirt.

For laughs, he once threw a string of firecrackers into the audience. Needless to say, these behaviors did not sit well with management. He was canned.

In other words, they made him an offer he couldn't refuse. For a final flourish, he exacted revenge by stuffing rotten Lim-

Marlon Brando once worked as an usher in this Libertyville theater.

burger cheese into the theater's ventilation system.

> *"Hey, Johnny, what are you rebelling against?"*
> *"What've you got?"*
> — *The Wild One*, 1953

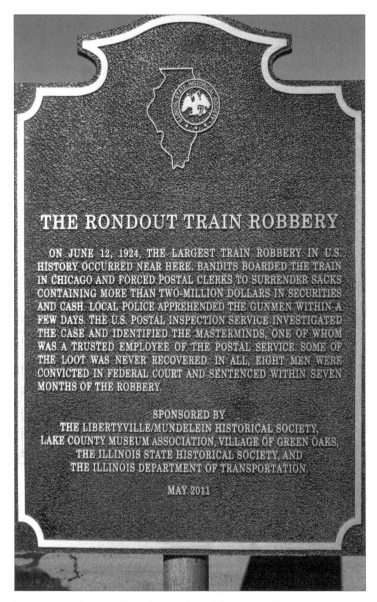

Memorial to the great Roundout Train Robbery—the biggest train robbery in United States history.

Indeed.
While You're Here:

As long as you're in this neck of the woods (the Libertyville area), a very short drive will take you to a remembrance of America's most brazen train robbery.

Bonus: The Great Rondout Train Robbery
13629 Rockland Road (Route 176), Lake Bluff IL 60044

Here you will find a small historical marker detailing the events (at least some of them) of June 12, 1924, (which actually took place a few miles north of this spot). On that date, a well-planned train robbery of $2 million in cash, jewelry and securities (the equivalent of $29 million in today's money) went down.

A train headed north from Chicago's Union Station was ordered to halt by two stowaway gunmen where the tracks crossed Route 137. Waiting in several Cadillacs there were four co-conspirators, who quickly loaded the loot into the cars.

The gang, including the four notorious Newton brothers (Willis, Joe, Willie & Jesse) might have gotten away with the crime except for one fatal mistake. Willie Newton was accidently shot by another member of the gang during the robbery. The others hurriedly loaded the bleeding Willie into one of the vehicles and drove off.

This mistake proved to be their undoing. Authorities quickly learned two things: (1) A man was being treated for a gunshot wound in Chicago, and (2), all the evidence clearly pointed to the crime being an "inside job."

Arrests were soon made, and convictions followed, including that of a postal inspector who supplied the gang with the detailed information needed for the plan.

Note: This crime definitely did not pay. However, not all of the loot was recovered. So, you might want to look around the area a bit.

Bonus: Harrison Ford/ Indiana Jones in Park Ridge

A little jog south will take you to Park Ridge and:

Harrison Ford's Boyhood Home
109 N. Washington Avenue, Park Ridge IL 60068
Technically, he should have been "Illinois Jones," but it doesn't really have quite the same ring, does it? Ford grew up in the 1950s in this modest Tudor-style brick home. Look for the upstairs balcony: the room it led to was Ford's.

Note: Hillary Rodham Clinton grew up in a home only a few blocks away.

Hillary Rodham Clinton

Hillary Rodham Clinton's Childhood Home
235 N. Wisner Street, Park Ridge IL 60068

Note: No more info. Loose lips sink ships.

John Belushi

John Belushi grew up in Wheaton. His comedic and musical talents blossomed while he was a member of Chicago's famed Second City troupe. He would go on to attain national fame as a member of Saturday Night Live before making a very successful transition to films. Animal House and The Blues Brothers established Belushi as a megastar, and a bright future seemed certain. Sadly, a penchant for self-destructive behavior cut his life short.

It all came crashing down on March 5, 1982. While staying in a bungalow at L.A.'s Chateau Marmont Hotel, Belushi overdosed on a deadly injection cocktail of heroin and cocaine. He was 33.

John Belushi's Boyhood Home: The Original Animal House
904 R. Elm Street, Wheaton IL 60189
The Belushi brothers grew up in this home. The family owned it from approximately 1953 to 1979. Neighbors would frequently be awakened at all hours of the night by the loud music emanating from the band practices conducted in the Belushi garage.

🔍*Note:* The home now looks considerably different from the way it did when the Belushi family lived here.

The Belushi Family Plot
And a Mystery (or The Plot Gets Thicker)
Elmwood Cemetery, 2905 Thatcher Avenue
River Grove IL 60171
There's long been a kind of mystery involving the grave of John Belushi. He was allegedly first interred in a marked grave at Abel Hill Cemetery in Martha's Vineyard.

When overzealous fans began paying a little too much attention to the grave, his wife had him reburied in an unmarked grave in a section of the same cemetery. The whole story has always seemed a bit odd.

Adam and Agnes Belushi, John's parents, are buried here in River Grove. I've always wondered if John himself rests nearby.

═══ Betty White ═══
218 Pleasant Street, Apartment 3A, Oak Park IL 60302

Betty White, the incredibly durable comedienne of countless TV shows and films, spent the first two years of her life here in Oak Park. She is probably best-remembered as a cast member on two megahits, *The Mary Tyler Moore Show* and *The*

Golden Girls. She lived in this apartment building with her parents, Horace, and Tess before the family relocated to Los Angeles.

Ernest Hemingway:
The Old Man and the Oak Park

Note: Hemingway was never an old man here; he pretty much left Oak Park for good at age 23. I just wanted to be cloyingly cute with *The Old Man and the Sea* reference.

Hemingway, one of the giants of modern American literature, was born here in Oak Park in 1899. The village has always struggled a bit with a quote attributed to him describing his birthplace as a place of "wide lawns and narrow minds."

"Papa" Hemingway would go on to author such classic novels as *The Sun Also Rises, A Farewell to Arms, For Whom the Bell Tolls* and *To Have and Have Not.*

Ernest Hemingway's Boyhood Home
339 N. Oak Park Avenue, Oak Park IL 60302
You can tour the home: Wednesdays through Sundays. Contact the Ernest Hemingway Birthplace Museum for details.

Mary Todd Lincoln:
Batty in Batavia
Bellevue Place, 333 S. Jefferson Street, Batavia IL 60510

Abraham's widow, Mary, had a rough time in the years following his assassination. In addition to that tragedy, she had already endured the early deaths of three of her four sons. Never noted for her mental stability even in the best of times, by 1875 her behavior had become so erratic and troubling that her surviving son, Robert, arranged for her to be committed to Bellevue Place, a "sanitarium for disturbed ladies" here in

Batavia. Mrs. Lincoln resided here for several months before being granted a second hearing, where she was deemed sane and released.

Note: Mrs. Lincoln resided on the second floor. Her estate was charged $10 per day for the room. As you face the entrance, her room would be the second floor, left. The building has now been converted into a private apartment complex.
Also:

Where she Lived in Chicago
1232 W. Washington Boulevard, Chicago IL 60607
Mary Todd Lincoln, following the assassination, moved to Chicago and settled in to a Washington Blvd. row house, where she lived with her son, Tad, for about a year. Desperate to pay off shopping debts she had concealed from her husband while in the White House, Mrs. Lincoln sold much of her furniture to a hotel.

Note: The house is no longer there.

Okay, back to the North Shore for more celebrity stuff!

Linda Darnell: B Star Tragedy in Glenview
75 Carriage Hill Drive, Glenview IL 60025

Linda Darnell appeared in lots of films, mostly in the 40s and 50s, but today few even seem to remember her name. A scan of her credits somewhat explains this: for every *Mark of Zorro* or *Blood and Sand*, which might trigger at least a tinge of recognition, there were a ton of other films I honestly had never heard of. She was a true member of the B movie star club; in the Hollywood star orbit, she would perhaps have been Saturn (and trending toward Pluto).

By 1965, her Tinseltown career was pretty much finished,

but she was still working. Darnell was staying at her secretary's townhome in Glenview while appearing in a local dinner playhouse production.

On the night of April 19, she watched one of her old films on television, then headed to bed around 2:30 AM. Around 5 AM a fire broke out in the downstairs living room. Awoken by smoke, her secretary and her teenage daughter exited the home from an upstairs window while Darnell headed downstairs to retrieve some important papers. Bad move. Overcome by the heat and smoke, she collapsed at the foot of the stairs.

Firemen arrived and carried Darnell from the home and to a local hospital. But there was little to be done; she had received third degree burns over 90% of her body.

Linda Darnell died the next day.

Note: The townhome was completely renovated after the tragic fire and remains occupied today.

Harold Ramis
160 Euclid Avenue, Glencoe IL 60022

Harold Ramis, despite a wildly successful career as writer, actor, and director of a ton of Hollywood blockbuster films, kept his feet firmly on the ground and remained true to his Chicago-area roots.

At the height of fame, he eschewed the Beverly Hills lifestyle, preferring to raise his family here in Glencoe. And from all accounts, he did his best to remain just a regular guy, navigating the village—and living his life—in a low-key manner and without fanfare.

Born in Chicago in 1944, Ramis joined the famed Second City troupe, then worked with the television show SCTV. His terrific writing and directing skills (as well as his comedy acting) were noticed, and his film career took off. The success of *Animal House, Meatballs, Stripes, National Lampoon's Vacation* and *Caddyshack* cemented his reputation as a top movie maker, and then the *Ghostbusters* and *Groundhog Day* hits made him a Hollywood force.

By 1996, Ramis now had the clout to do whatever he wanted—wherever he wanted—and he chose to live with his family back on the North Shore in this home and pursue projects that were often a bit more on the eclectic side and not as commercially viable as previous ones.

From 2010 on, however, his health began to decline. He passed away on February 24, 2014.

Note: In 2015, Ramis's family put the home up for sale. According to a realtor, the basement contained cardboard boxes filled with Ramis's original movie scripts, as well as a belt from the hit *Ghostbusters*, still smeared with residual white goop from the marshmallow man.

Michael Jordan:
"Look on my works, ye Mighty, and Despair."
2700 Point Lane, Highland Park IL 60035

How about a home that reeks of wretched excess? It's this one. Chicago Bulls basketball star Michael Jordan lived here during his reign as (arguably) the greatest hoops player of all time. Apparently, he wanted everyone to know it. Imagine a 56,000 square-foot mansion, complete with swimming pool (with an island in the middle!), regulation-size indoor basketball court, fully-equipped gym, tennis courts, and putting green. Oh, and 19 bathrooms.

Jordan and his first wife raised their kids here until their 2006 divorce. MJ got the mansion in the settlement, and has been trying to unload it for a long, long time. Since the asking price was originally only $29 million, I'm surprised it wasn't snapped up.

You are not going to really get all that close to the place; just look for the modest, giant "23" on the locked front gates.

Robin Williams
460 N. Washington Road, Lake Forest IL 60045

Comic, TV star, and movie icon Robin Williams was born in Chicago in 1951 and spent his formative years at this house in Lake Forest (the family moved to Detroit in 1963). Former classmates and friends recall him as funny, quick-witted, and constantly carrying on conversations with himself using a variety of improvised voices.

He attended nearby Gorton Elementary School and Deerpath Middle School.

Williams went on to star in the smash TV hit *Mork & Mindy* before achieving movie stardom with such films as *Popeye, Good Morning, Vietnam, Dead Poets Society, Good Will Hunting* and *Mrs. Doubtfire.*

He died in 2014.

Note: The home is still here.

Fred Savage
151 Park Avenue, Glencoe IL 60022

Fred Savage, born in 1976, lived here in Glencoe with his family while pursuing an acting career, which began with a failed audition for a hot dog commercial. His big break came with his appearance as Peter Falk's grandson in the film *The Princess Bride*, in 1987. The lead role (Kevin Arnold) in the hit TV series *The Wonder Years* soon followed.

Savage soon left the North Shore for California, but has remained close with the area friends he grew up with, returning frequently for visits.

He has continued an acting, producing and directing career in both the film and TV mediums.

Note: The home is still here.

Mr. T
395 Green Bay Road, Lake Forest IL 60045

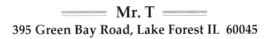

This Lake Forest mansion, known as the Twin Gables, was once owned by the Armour family, the Chicago meat-packing magnates.

In 1986, it was sold to flamboyant actor Laurence Tureaud—better known as Mr. T. Rocketing to stardom with his portrayal of boxer "Clubber Lang" in 1982's *Rocky 3*, Tureaud soon landed a major role on the hit TV show, *The A Team*.

Now famous and flush with cash, Mr. T. decided to return to his Chicago area roots and purchased the Twin Gables. In 1987, for reasons still unclear, he decided to indulge in a bit of somewhat radical landscaping: an action still often referred to as "The Lake Forest Chainsaw Massacre."

Wielding a chainsaw, the actor cut down over 100 stately oaks, elms and maples that lined the sprawling seven and a half-acre estate. Lake Forest residents were outraged by this latest affront to their community. (Mr. T had previously tried to erect an enormous "T" gate fronting his property, but was stopped). Lawsuits flew, and stringent laws were soon on the suburb's books, forbidding any future nature transgressions.

In 1993, Mr. T transferred the property deed to a girlfriend, and in 1999 it was sold. The wealthy townsfolk of Lake Forest breathed a collective sigh of relief.

Note: The Twin Gables estate has been replanted with 150 new trees.

John Hughes
855 E. Westminster, Lake Forest IL 60045

I've got to admit up front that I was never a fan of director John Hughes's films. With the exception of the *National Lampoon Vacation* series and *Planes, Trains and Automobiles*, their appeal and my tastes were separated by at least a one and a half-generation gap.

Still, the bits and pieces of his other films (*Ferris Bueller's Day Off, Home Alone, Pretty in Pink, Sixteen Candles, Uncle Buck, Dennis the Menace*) I caught while channel-surfing, always seemed rather nice, good-natured, albeit teen-based fare. Not *Citizen Kane* stuff for sure, but … pleasant.

One rather cool thing about Hughes was that he based an awful lot of his stories here on the North Shore. He had moved here from Michigan while in seventh grade, and seemed to really take to the area.

He lived here in Lake Forest until suddenly passing away from a heart attack at age 59 in 2009.

Here is a list of a few movie scenes that were filmed nearby:

Home Alone *House. 671 Lincoln Avenue, Winnetka, IL 60093*
Maccauley Culkin ("Kevin McAllister") and family lived here.

Ferris Bueller's Day Off: *Cameron's Home. 370 Beech St., Highland Park IL 60035*
Ferris's buddy, Cameron, lived here. His garage played a crucial role.

Planes, Trains, and Automobiles: *Steve Martin ("Neal Page") Home. 230 Oxford Road, Kenilworth IL 60043*
"Neal" (Steve Martin) brought John Candy here for Thanksgiving.

Dennis the Menace: *House of Mr. Wilson (Walter Matthau). 1618 Ashland Avenue, Evanston IL 60201*
Dennis' house is next door.

Note: Good news for you if you are a Hughes fan—there are lots more filming locations in the area. Look 'em up!

Robert Reed

Actor Robert Reed was a troubled soul, both professionally and personally. He longed to be perceived and remembered as a serious dramatic actor, yet he found his legacy would forever identify him as "Mike Brady," the affable, oddly-permed father on *The Brady Bunch*, perhaps the sappiest TV sitcom of all time.

Personally, he struggled with his sexuality. Although married from 1954 to 1959, Reed finally at some point accepted the fact that he was gay. He did live in fear of being outed, believing it would ruin his career.

Reed was born in Highland Park and spent his early years in Des Plaines. He died in 1992 from colon cancer, compromised by being HIV-positive. His body was brought back to the North Shore for burial.

Note: His tombstone reads, "Good Night Sweet Prince."

Robert Reed's Des Plaines Boyhood Home
621 Parsons Ave, Des Plaines IL 60016

His Grave: Mike Brady's Last Stop in Skokie
Memorial Park Cemetery, 9900 Gross Point Road, Skokie IL
60076 Annex 6, Lot 21

Harry Caray

Harry Caray's Grave: "Holy Cow!"
All Saints Catholic Cemetery, 700 N. River Road
Des Plaines IL 60016. Section 42W, Block 22, Lot 13, Grave 4

Legendary baseball broadcaster Harry Caray was at various times the voice of the St. Louis Cardinals, Oakland A's and Chicago White Sox, but it was his stint announcing the games of the Chicago Cubs (beginning with the 1982 season) that forever cemented his image as a national celebrity. Caray's flamboyant style kept Cub fans engaged and entertained throughout many dismal, losing seasons.

Caray was instrumental in popularizing the singing of *Take Me Out to the Ballgame* during seventh inning stretches.

He passed away in 1990.

⚲*Note:* Caray once said: "Sure as God made green apples, someday, the Cubs are going to be in the World Series." When the Cubs made it at last to the Series in 2016, fans decorated his grave with caseloads of green apples.

The Villa Venice:
The Rat Pack in … Wheeling?
2855 N. Milwaukee Avenue, Chicago IL 60062

Frank Sinatra sure seemed forever indebted to the Chicago Outfit—and boss Sam Giancana, in particular. Maybe that story in the Godfather (a mob boss got a popular singer out of an unfavorable contract by holding a gun to a bandleader's head) was true. Or maybe, Ol' Blue Eyes was mightily grateful to Giancana and his friends for their rumored help in swinging the 1960 presidential election to John F. Kennedy.

Whatever the reason, Sinatra in 1962 persuaded his Rat Pack buddies, Dean Martin and Sammy Davis Jr., to join him for a week-long stint in … Las Vegas? No. Tahoe? Nope. Reno? Uh uh. Drumroll, please … Wheeling!

Here's the skinny: Sinatra's supposed close goombah, Momo Giancana, owned a large piece of the Villa Venice, a large restaurant/nightclub located beside the Des Plaines River in Wheeling. The venue itself was more or less a front; the real money came not from lobster tails and highballs—it came from illegal gambling, conducted at a Quonset hut located a few blocks away. High-rollers would be shuttled from the restaurant to this location long into the night.

By 1962, Giancana was looking to attract bigger crowds. Even though no expense had been spared on opulence—patrons were treated to gondola rides on the Des Plaines River—piloted by singing boatmen!—more gamblers were needed. Giancana decided that a big-name act was required to draw the suckers. And Sinatra owed him.

On November 26, 1962, the Rat Pack began their Villa Ven-

The mob-controlled Villa Venice Nightclub once stood here along the Des Plaines River on Milwaukee Avenue. The Site is now occupied by a different venue.

ice engagement, and for one week, Wheeling, Illinois was the hottest address in show business. A newspaper nightlife critic described the events in this distinctly old-school way: Frank, Dean and Sammy "croon, carol, caper and clown to the biggest cabaret audiences this town has seen in years."

Giancana's ploy was a huge success. The Villa Venice (and the Outfit) raked in major cash during that week. But the good fortune didn't last. Profits eventually began to steadily decline, and Giancana apparently decided to pull the plug.

In 1965, the Villa Venice changed ownership hands. In 1967, it burned to the ground in a mysterious fire.

It's unknown if Sinatra, Martin and Davis ever were paid for their services, or if this was strictly a favor to Giancana and the Outfit. (A favor they couldn't refuse?) One telling quote from Davis, years later, is instructive: "I got one eye, and that one eye sees a lot of things my brain tells me I shouldn't talk about. Because my brain says that, if I do, my one eye might not be seeing anything after a while."

🔍 *Note:* The Villa Venice has been replaced with All-gauer's Restaurant and the Hilton Northbrook, but it's still possible to walk around the site and imagine bygone showbiz splendor.

7. FURTHER READING AND REFERENCES

There are *tons* of books dealing with the iconic "biggies" of Chicago area weird stuff. Over the years, I have waded through just about all of them.

Here are the a few of the really indispensable ones I would heartily recommend:

• Seltzer, Adam (2016). *Mysterious Chicago.* New York: Sky-horse Publishing.

• Seltzer, Adam (2013). *The Ghosts of Chicago.* Woodbury, MN: Llewellyn Publications. (Selzer is great. He delivers the goods without the nonsense).

• Lindberg, Richard (1999). *Return to the Scene of the Crime.* Nashville: Cumberland House Publishing. (Lindberg's research is exhaustive—and he's a very nice guy).

• Lindberg, Richard (2001). *Return AGAIN to the Scene of the Crime.* Nashville: Cumberland House Publishing.

• Schechter, Harold (1998). *Deviant.* New York: Simon & Schuster. (I chose this book because it's my favorite one by Schechter, but anything this guy writes is terrific).

•   Baumann, Ed & O'Brien, John (1991). *Getting Away With Murder* (1991) Chicago: Bonus Books, Inc.

Additional References

Newspaper Articles

Allen, Jim. May 29, 2008. Police still optimistic on solving Brown's murders. *Daily Herald.*

Associated Press. July 19, 2017. Timeline of John Wayne Gacy's case. *Daily Herald.*

Banas, Casey. September 10, 1985. Hefner Back to Retrace the Bunny Trail. *Chicago Tribune.*

Bannon, Tim. July 23, 2019. George Halas was supposed to be on the SS Eastland the day it capsized in the Chicago River, killing 844 people. *Chicago Tribune.*

Baumann, Edward & O'Brien, John. August 3, 1986. "The Sausage Factory Mystery." *Chicago Tribune.*

Baumann, Jim. May 24, 2019. There's nothing for these paramedics to do: Remembering the Flight 191 Crash. *Daily Herald.*

Beard, David. October 20, 1995. Death of a Secret. *South Florida Sun Sentinel.*

Bernard Megan. April 18, 2018. Fred, Ben Savage's childhood home hits the real estate market in Glencoe. *The Glencoe Anchor.*

Black, Lisa. January 2, 2015. New look at Rouse murders stirs chilling memories. *Chicago Tribune.*

Borelli, Christopher. November 11, 2013. Bruce Dern's long run to Nebraska. *Chicago Tribune.*

Bovsun, Mara. August 22, 2009. Twisted Sister. *New York Daily News.*

Carlozo, Lou. January 2, 1995. Rouse Son's Confession: "Everybody Knew." *Chicago Tribune.*

Chicago Catholic. 2018. Tragic Our Lady of the Angels School fire recalled 60 years later.

Constable, Burt. April 21, 2018. Constable: 71-year-old man believes he could have been one of Gacy's first victims." *Daily Herald.*

Constable, Burt. November 26, 2019. Constable: Impact of mob in suburbs mostly memories, but not to FBI. *Daily Herald.*

Crosby, Denise. October 29, 2011. Ghost experts dig into local folktale…and the plot thickens. *Naperville Sun.*

Daday, Eileen. February 18, 2008. Retired detective to discuss 1950's murders with 2002 conviction. *Daily Herald.*

Daniels, Mary. October 29, 2006. The haunting legends of Lobstein House. *Chicago Tribune.*

Dizikes, Cynthia. November 25, 2011. Ruby ring may hold clue to 1977 disappearance of heiress. *Chicago Tribune.*

Dudek, Mitch. December 14, 2018. Where John Wayne Gacy buried the bodies, more; key sites tied to serial killer. *Chicago Sun-Times.*

Filas, Lee. May 18, 2017. "I can still smell that crime scene:" Ray Rose recalls 50-year career. *Daily Herald.*

Franklin, Shaffer. October 9, 2018. Ghost Stories #2: The Forest Scout/Lake Forest High School.

Goldsborough, Bob. June 8, 2015. Harold Ramis' Glencoe mansion sell for $2.3 million. *Chicago Tribune.*

Griffin, Jean Latz & McMahon, Colin. July 26, 1991. Suspect's Behavior Raised Few Questions, Chicago Bar Patrons Say. *Chicago Tribune.*

Grossman, Ron. December 4, 2015. Chicago Mob boss had Sinatra singing. *Chicago Tribune.*

Grumman, Cornelia. January 2, 1995. Son Confesses to 1980 Slaying Of Parents. *Chicago Tribune.*

Hilkevitch, Jon & O'Brien, Margaret. February 9, 2000. Bob Collins Dies In Plane Collision. *Chicago Tribune.*

Janega, James; Maxwell, Tonya & Peters, Alan. August 9, 2007. '57 cold case is rekindled. *Chicago Tribune.*

Johnson, Jennifer. August 1, 2015. 41 years later, Park Ridge family's murder still remembered. *Chicago Tribune.*

Keilman, John. January 8, 2013. Brown's Chicken killings : 20 years ago today.

Chicago Tribune.

Kogan, Rick. March 1, 1994. Homecoming. *Chicago Tribune.*

Kogan, Rick. August 7, 2005. Wise Guy. *Chicago Tribune.*

Krishnamurthy, Madhu. May 25, 2016. First responders recollect chilling visions of Flight 191 crash. *Daily Herald.*

Lawton, Mark. July 13, 2016. A century later, Lake Forest murder trial still fascinates. Pioneer Press.

Lyon, Jeff. July 8, 1985. Benny Goodman. *Chicago Tribune.*

Maier, Thomas. April 6, 2019. Mafia Spies: Sam Giancana is gunned down before he can be called before Senate. *Chicago Sun-Times.*

Maier, Thomas. April 5, 2019. Mafia Spies: Why mob boss Sam Giancana made Rat Pack play his Northbrook Club. *Chicago Sun-Times.*

Mount, Charles. July 24, 1992. Grisly Tale Unfolds As Church Enters Guilty Plea. *Chicago Tribune.*

Obejas, Achy. October 5, 2000. L. Frank Baum – The Man Behind 'The Wizard Of Oz'—Was Really the Man Behind the Curtain. *Chicago Tribune.*

O'Brien, John. February 14, 2014. The St. Valentine's Day Massacre. *Chicago Tribune.*

O'Brien, John & Martin, Andrew. August 6, 1997. Cunanan Print Confirmed at Miglin Home. *Chicago Tribune.*

Olmstead, Rob. August 29, 2007. Mob trial closings about 'lies and deception'. *Daily Herald.*

Phillips, Michael. August 13, 2018. Seven things to know about actress Kim Novak and 'Vertigo'. *Chicago Tribune.*

Rodkin, Dennis. November 3, 2019. A yellow brick road honors 'Oz' author on site of his home. *Crain's Chicago Business.*

Roeder, David. May 24, 2019. O'Hare western access tollway planned for field where Flight 191 crashed 40 years ago. *Chicago Sun-Times.*

Sadin, Steve. October 18, 2013. Michael Jordan To Auction Highland Park Mansion. *Patch: Wilmette/Kenilworth.*

Shales, Tom. October 14, 1996. Kim Novak: No Fear of Falling. *The Washington Post.*

Smith, Wes. May 10, 1987. An Old Haunt Gets A New Lease On Life. *Chicago Tribune.*

Sotonoff, Jamie. August 1, 2011. Attorney: John Wayne Gacy had a 34th victim." *Daily Herald.*

Swanson, Lorraine. July 14, 2016. Born to Raise Hell. Prosecutor Revisits Richard Speck Mass Murders on 50th Anniversary. *Patch/Patch Media.*

Tarapacki, Thomas. November 18, 2019. The man that Al Capone feared. *The Am-Pol Eagle.*

The Editors. January 28, 2018. Cunanan's Murders. *Cosmopolitan.*

The New York Times. July 19, 1974. Son's Death Studied After 4 in Family Are Slain."

Villareal, Yvonne. July 22, 2013. Dennis Farina dies at 69; Chicago police officer turned actor. *L.A. Times.*

Wessel, Todd. March 21, 2011. Actor Robert Reed Grew Up In Des Plaines; Biographer Looking For More Clues. *Journal & Topics.*

Wilmington, Michael. December 19, 2007. Essanay Studios. *Chicago Tribune.*

Winter, Christine. September 27, 1995. Bull Valley Home Haunted only by Reputation. *Chicago Tribune.*

Zumbach, Lauren. May 23, 2019. The Legacy of Flight 191. *Chicago Tribune.*

Zwecker, Bill. December 7, 2015. Michael Gross has two very different reunions. *Chicago Sun-Times.*

Archival Newspaper Articles

The Park Ridge Herald. Vol. 81, No. 10. March 9, 1967. Aftermath Here of 'Box' Tragedy.

Park Ridge Advocate. Vol. XXXII, No. 49. March 9, 1967. No Date Yet Set For Inquest Into Death Of Burglar.

Sowa, Tony. March 2, 1967. The Perfect Crime: Youth Ends Own Life. *Chicago Tribune.*

Books

Abbott, Karen. 2007. *Sin in the Second City: Madams, Minister, Playboys and the Battle for America's Soul.* New York: Random House.

Alaspa, Brian. 2010. *Silas Jayne: Chicago's Suburban Gangster.* Charleston, SC: The History Press.

Allen, Steve. 1960. *Mark It and Strike It: An Autobiography.* New York: Holt, Rinehart & Winston.

Amirante, Sam. 2015. *John Wayne Gacy: Defending a Monster: The True Story of the Lawyer Who Defended One of the Most Evil Serial Killers in History.* New York: Skyhorse Publishing.

Altman, Jack & Ziporyn, Marvin. 1967. *Born to Raise Hell: The Untold Story of Richard Speck - The Man, The Crime, The Trial.* New York: Grove Press.

Ashbury, Herbert. 2002. *The Gangs of Chicago.* New York: Basic Books.

Baumann, Ed & O'Brien, John. 1991. *Getting Away with Murder.* Chicago: Bonus Books, Inc.

Bielski, Ursula & Hucke, Matt. 1999. *Graveyards of Chicago: The People, History, Art & Lore of Cook County Cemeteries.* Chicago: Lake Claremont Press.

Bielski, Ursula. 2000. *More Chicago Haunts.* Chicago: Lake Claremont Press.

Borowski, John. 2016. *The Ed Gein File A Psycho's Confession and Case Documents.* Chicago: Waterfront Productions.

Borowski, John. 2005. *The Strange Case of Dr. H. H. Holmes.* Waterfront Productions.

Breo, Dennis, & Martin, William. 1993 and 2016. *The Crime of the Century: Richard Speck and the Murders That Shocked a Nation.* New York: Skyhorse Publishing.

Brooks, Rachel. 2008. Chicago Ghosts. Atglen, PA: Schiffer Publishing, Ltd.

Cahill, Tim. 1987. *Buried Dreams: Inside the Mind of a Serial Killer.* New York: Bantam.

Clearfield, Dylan. 1997. *Chicagoland Ghosts* © 1997 by Garry Stempien. Holt, MI: Thunder Bay Press, 1997

Coen, Jeff. 2010. *Family Secrets: The Case That Crippled The Chicago Mob.* Chicago: Chicago Review Press.

Cowan, David. 1998. *To Sleep with the Angels.* Chicago: Ivan R. Dee.

Crowe, Richard. 2000. *Chicago's Street Guide To The Supernatural.* Oak Park ,IL: Carolando Press, Inc.

Cullota, Frank & Griffin, Dennis N. 2007. *The Rise and Fall of a 'Casino' Mobster: The Tony Spilotro Story Through a Hitman's Eyes.* Denver: WildBlue Press.

Dark, Tony. 2008. *A Mob of His Own: Mad Sam DeStefano and the Chicago Mob's "Juice" Rackets.* Hosehead Productions.

Dern, Bruce; Crane, Robert; and Fryer, Christopher. 2007. *Things I've Said, But Probably Shouldn't Have: An Unrepentant Memoir.* Hoboken: Wiley.

Egginton, Joyce. 1991. *Day of Fury: The Story of the Tragic Shootings That Forever Changed the Village of Winnetka.* New York: William Morrow & Co.

Eghigian Jr., Mars. 2005. *After Capone: The Life and World of Chicago Mob Boss Frank "The Enforcer" Nitti.* Nashville: Cumberland House Publishing.

Eig, Jonathan. 2010. *Get Capone.* New York: Simon & Schuster.

Englade, Ken. 1996. *Hot Blood: The Money, the Brach Heiress, the Horse Murders.* New York: St. Martin's Press.

Frantz, Kevin J. 2009. *Naperville, Chicago's Haunted Neighbor.* Monee, Illinois: Unrested Dead Publishing.

Frantz, Kevin. 2012. *The Grave Robber Next Door … A Love Story: The true story behind Naperville's most notorious secret.* Monee, Illinois: Unrested Dead Publishing.

Giancana, Sam & Burnstein, Scott. 2010. *Family Affair: Greed, Treachery, and Betrayal in the Chicago Mafia.* New York: Penguin Group.

Giancana, Sam, Giancana, Chuck & Giancana, Bettina. 2014. *Double Cross: The Explosive Inside Story of the Mobster Who Controlled America.* New York: Skyhorse Publishing.

Green, Ryan. 2019. *The Townhouse Massacre: The Unforgettable Crimes of Richard Speck.* Independently Published.

Griffith, William. 2013. *American Mafia: Chicago: True Stories of Families Who Made Windy City History.* Guilford, CT: Globe Pequot.

Gusfield, Jeffrey. 2016 (Reprint Edition). *Deadly Valentines: The Story of Capone's Henchman "Machine Gun" Jack McGurn and Louise Rolfe, His Blonde Alibi.* Chicago: Chicago Review Press.

Helmer, William & Bilek, Arthur. 2004. *The St. Valentine's Day Massacre: The Untold Story of the Gangland Bloodbath that Brought Down Al Capone.* Nashville:

Cumberland House Publishing.

Heston, Charlton. 1978. *The Actor's Life.* New York: E.P. Dutton.

Howard, Clark. 1993. *Love's Blood.* New York: St. Martin's Press.

Iorizzo, Luciano. 2003. *Al Capone: A Biography.* Westport, CT: Greenberg Publishing Group.

Jack, James A. 2006. *Three Boys Missing: The Tragedy That Exposed The Pedophilia Underworld.* Chicago: HPH Pub.

Johnson, Raymond. 2013. *Chicago History: The Stranger Side.* Atglen, PA: Schiffer Publishing, Ltd.

Johnson, Wayne. 2014. *A History of Violence: An Encyclopedia of 1400 of Chicago Mob Murders.* LLR Books-Leader.

Kaplan, James. 2015. *Sinatra: The Chairman.* New York: Anchor Books.

Kaplan, Joel. 1990. *Murder of Innocence: The Tragic Life and Final Rampage of Laurie Dann, the Schoolhouse Killer.* New York: Warner Books.

Kaczmarek, Dale. 2000. *Windy City Ghosts.* Alton, IL: Whitechapel Productions Press.

Keefe, Rose. 2003. *Guns and Roses: The Untold Story of Dean O'Banion, Chicago's Big Shot Before Al Capone.* Nashville: Cumberland House Publishing.

Keefe, Rose. 2005. *The Man Who Got Away: The Bugs Moran Story: A Biography.* Nashville: Cumberland House Publishing.

Ladley, Diane A. 2009. *Haunted Naperville.* Charleston, SC: Arcadia Publishing.

Lewis, Chad & Fisk, Terry. 2007. *The Illinois Road Guide to Haunted Locations.* Eau Claire, WI: Unexplained Research Pub. Co.

Lindberg, Richard. 2001. *Return AGAIN to the Scene of the Crime.* Nashville: Cumberland House Publishing.

Lindberg, Richard. 1999. *Return to the Scene of the Crime.* Nashville: Cumberland House Publishing.

Lindberg, Richard C. & Sykes, Gloria Jean. 2006. *Shattered Sense of Innocence.* Carbondale, IL: Southern Illinois University Press.

Loerzel, Robert. 2007. *Alchemy of Bones: Chicago's Luetgert Murder Case of 1897.* Champaign, IL: University of Illinois Press.

Markus, Scott. 2008. *Voices from the Chicago Grave.* Holt, MI: Thunder Bay Press.

Medved, Harry & Medved, Michael. 1984. *The Hollywood Hall Of Shame: The Most Expensive Flops In Movie History.* New York: Perigree Books/The Putnam Publishing Group.

Miller, Donald L. 1997. *City of the Century: The Epic of Chicago and the Making of America.* New York: Simon & Schuster.

Morris, Jeff & Shields, Vince. 2013. *Chicago Haunted Handbook.* Covington, KY: Clerisy Press.

Reed, Jaymes. 2011. *Comics: The Three Stooges.* Vancouver, WA: Bluewater Productions.

Remsberg, Bonnie. 1992. *Mom, Dad, Mike & Pattie: The True Story of the Columbo Murders.* New York: Bantam.

Roemer, William. 1995. *Accardo: The Genuine Godfather.* New York: Ivy Books.

Roemer Jr., William. 1995. *The Enforcer: Spilotro: The Chicago Mob's Man Over Las Vegas.* New York: Ivy Books.

Schechter, Harold. 1998. *Deviant.* New York: Simon & Schuster.

Shmelter, Richard J. 2008. *Chicago Assassin: The Life and Legend of Machine Gun Jack McGurn and the Chicago Beer Wars of the Roaring Twenties.* Nashville: Cumberland House Publishing.

Schoenberg, Robert J. 1993. *Mr. Capone: The Real – and Complete – Story of Al Capone.* New York: William Morrow Paperbacks, Reprint Edition.

Selzer, Adam. 2017. *H.H. Holmes: The True Story of the White City Devil.* New York: Skyhorse Publishing.

Selzer, Adam. 2016. *Mysterious Chicago.* New York: Skyhorse Publishing.

Selzer, Adam. 2013. *The Ghosts of Chicago.* Woodbury, MN. Llewelyn Publications.

Shaffer, Tamara. 2006. *Murder Gone Cold: The Mystery of the Grimes Sisters.* Ghost Research Society.

Taylor, Troy. 2015. *The Two Lost Girls: The Mystery of the Grimes Sisters.* Jacksonville, IL: Whitechapel Press/American Hauntings, Inc.

Thompson, Emily G. 2018. *Unsolved Child Murders: Eighteen American Cases 1956-1998.* Jefferson, NC: Exposit.

Sullivan, Terry & Maiken, Peter. 2013. *Killer Clown*. Chicago: Pinnacle Books.

Ylisela, James Jr. 2014. *Who Killed the Candy Lady? Unwrapping the Unsolved Murder of Helen Brach.* Evanston, IL: Agate Digital.

Web Sites

Alaspa, Bryan. 2010. *A Chicago Unsolved Murder: Judith Mae Anderson.* The Crime Times. https://thecrimetimes.wordpress.com.

American Hauntings Ink. 2013. *The Girl in the Snow.* http://troytaylorbooks. blogspot.com.

American Mafia History. 2015. *'Machine Gun' Jack McGurn – St. Valentine's Day Massacre.* https://americanmafiahistory.com.

Amoruso, David. 2010. *Chicago Soldier: 'Mad Sam' DeStefano.* Gangsters, Inc. http://gangstersinc.ning.com.

Burkholder, Alex. 2018. *60 Years Later: Our Lady of the Angels School Fire.* Firehouse. https://www.firehouse.com.   .

Burns, Ken. 2004. *Unforgivable Blackness.* PBS. https://pbs.org.

Caddie Hall of Fame. 2015. *Murray Brothers.* WGA Site. https://caddiehalloffame.org.

Craig, Jim. 2015. *The Villa Venice: Albert 'Papa' Bouche.* Under Every Tombstone. http:/undereverytombstone.blogspot.com.

Danna, Jeff. 2010. *Mob's Influence Extended up Milwaukee Avenue.* Wheeling Historical Society and Museum. http://www.wheelinghistoricalsociety.com.

Darkes, Chris. August 4, 2014. *The Unstable Horseman.* Medium. https:/medium.com

De Sturler, Alice. February 1, 2016. *Case of the Month: Barbara and Patricia Grimes.* Defrosting Cold Cases. https://defrostingcoldcases.com.

Doorey, Marie. 2019. *Richard Speck American Murderer.* Encyclopedia Britannica. https://www.britannica.com.

Dretske, D. October 14, 2011. *Gangsters Bring Prohibition Violence to Fox Lake.* Lake County Illinois History. http:/www./lakecountyhistory.blogspot.com.

Ebert, Roger. 1992. *Hugh Hefner Returns to Halls and Haunts of a Chicago Childhood.* RogerEbert.com. https://www.rogerebert.com.

Elbert, Lisa. Undated. *L & L Tavern.* Thrillist. https://www.thrillist.com.

Erwin, Blane. 2017. *The Haunted History of the Red Geranium.* NCTV17, 2017. https://www.nctv17.com.

Figliulo, Susan. May 18, 2000. *The Marx Brothers' House.* Chicago Reader. https://www.nctv17.com.

Find A Grave. https://www.findagrave.com.

Gallo, Kenny. 2015. *Rouse Mansion: Murder, Corruption and a Casino.* Breakshot Blog. http://breakshotblog.blogspot.com

George Stickney House. December 16, 2019. Atlas Obscura. https://www.atlasobscura.com.

Goad, Jim. June 5, 2008. *8 Dead Nurses in One Night: The Horrible Story of Richard Speck.* Thought Catalog. https://thoughtcatalog.com.

Gomes, Mario. Undated. My Al Capone Museum. http://www.myalcaponemuseum.com.

Gribben, Mark. Undated. *Family Secrets.* The Malefactor's Register. http://malefactorsregister.com.

Google My Maps. Undated. *Murder 1957 – Judith Mae Anderson.* https://www.google.com.

Griffin, Simon. 2019. *10 Mysteries Involving Families.* ListVerse. https://listverse.com.

Heirens, William, Case. 2000. Newspaper Clippings, Special Collections Research Center. U. of Chicago Library. https://www.lib.uchicago.edu.

Higginbotham, Adam. 2008. *The Long, Long Life of the Lipstick Killer.* GQ Magazine. https://www.gq.com.

History in Glenview: The Brach Heiress. Undated. No author. Domu. https://www.domu.com.

History in Lakeview. Undated. No author. Domu. https://www.domu.com

Hogan, Stephen. Undated. Chicago Crime Scene Photos, Flickr. https://www.flickr.com

Huff, Andrew. 2004. *Sam Giancana's Last Meal.* Gapers Block. http://www.gapersblock.com.

IL-Judith Anderson, 15, Chicago – 16 August, 1957. 2007. Websleuths. https://www.websleuths.com.

Joe. February 16, 2017. *A Kid Named Bud: Marlon Brando in Libertyville, 1938-41.* Shelf Life, Cook Memorial Public Library District Blog. https://shelflife.cook-lib.org.

Johnson, Ray. 2017. *59th Anniversary of the Murder of Bonnie Leigh Scott of Addison Could Lead to Closure in the 1956 Grimes Sisters Murder.* Chicago History Cop. http://www.chicagonow.com.

JV. 2017. *The Grimes Sisters.* The Theorem Factory. https:/theoremfact.wordpress.com.

Leonard, Mike. 2018. *A Look Back at the Hubbard Woods School Shooting.* Chicago Magazine. https://www.chicagomag.com.

Logan, Malcolm. 2011. *Houses of Horror: The Serial Murder Sites of Chicago and Milwaukee.* My American Odyssey. http://myamericanodyssey.com.

Lunde, Anne. 2016. *Family Ties Strengthened by Discovery of Headstones.*Journal & Topics. www.journal-topics.com.

Mallon, Bridget. 2015. *Now's Your Chance to Tour the Chicago Home of Beloved Director John Hughes.* House Beautiful. https://www.housebeautiful.com.

Meacham, J.D. 1996. *The Lone Ranger: Home on the Range.* Edgewater Historical Society. www.edgewaterhistory.org.

Miller, Julie. 2018. *The Assassination of Gianni Versace: The Mysterious Murder of Lee Miglin.* Vanity Fair. www.vanityfair.com.

Mors, Terry. Volume 21, Number 2, 2018. *The Rouse House Revisited: Unraveling the Enigma of Murder, Police Corruption, and Organized Crime.* Casino Chip and Token News. URL not available.

Murderpedia.org. www.murderpedia.org.

Musto, Michael. April 25, 2012. *The Least Convincing Couple in Screen History.* The Village Voice. www.villagevoice.com.

NBC5Chicago. 2017. *50 Celebrities You Might Not Know Were from The Chicago Area.* www.nbcchicago.com.

Nitkin, Alex. 2018. *Dunning School Construction May Hit Dead Bodies, and the City is Planning for it.* Curbed Chicago. https://chicago.curbed.com.

Overton, Karen Anne. 2016. *What About Bill?* Sheridan Road Magazine. https://jwcdaily.com.

Pantagraph. 1957 clipping posted 2016. *Ax, Towel, Rag Newest Findings In Murder Case.* Newspapers.com. www.newspapers.com.

Pfeifer, Kelsey Grace. 2017. *10 Things You Need to Know About the Original Playboy Mansion In Chicago.* Culture Trip. https://theculturetrip.com.

Restoring Walt Disney's Birthplace. 2013. No author. Walt Disney's Birthplace. www.thewaltdisneybirthplace.org.

Rhoads, Mark. 2006. *Illinois Hall of Fame: Ann-Margret.* Illinois Review. www.illinoisreview.com.

Rhoads, Mark. June 22, 2006. *Illinois Hall of fame: The Marx Brothers.* Illinois Review. www.illinoisreview.com.

Rodkin, Dennis. 2009. *Lake Forest's Schweppe Mansion.* Chicago Magazine. www.chicagomag.com.

Rogan, Maura. 2004. *Rock Hudson: In Winnetka, We Call Him Roy.* Winnetka Historical Society. www.winnetkahistory.org.

Roman, Marisa. 2016. *You May Be Surprised to Learn These 15 Famous People are from Chicago.* Only in Your State. www.onlyinyourstate.com.

Ruiz, Mariah. 2016. *My Visit to the George Stickney House.* https://thegeorgestickneyhousemariahruiz.blogspot.com.

Selzer, Adam. 2016. *Excavating the H.H. Holmes' Body Dump Site.* Mysterious Chicago Tours. http://mysteriouschicago.com.

Selzer, Adam. 2009. *Old Town Tatu.* Mysterious Chicago Tours. http://mysteriouschicago.com/old-town-tatu.

Serena, Katie. 2018. *William Heirens was 17 When He was Convicted for Beheading a 6-Year-Old Girl – But Did He Do It?* All That's Interesting. https://allthatsinteresting.com.

Silver, Carley. 2019. *Sam Giancana: Chicago Godfather, CIA Collaborator, and the Man Who may have Put JFK In the White House.* All That's Interesting. https://allthatsinteresting.com.

Smith, Bryan. 2019. *The Ghosts of Flight 191.* Chicago Magazine. www.chicagomag.com.

Smith, Bryan. 2007. *House of Cards.* Chicago Magazine. www.chicagomag.com.

Starr, Steve. Undated. *Gloria Swanson.* Compass Rose Cultural Crossroads.. http://compassrose.org.

Stompanato, Lana. 2006. *Patty Columb—he Baddest Girl in Chicago's Northwest Suburbs."* The Power Dump Diaries. https://laswansong.blogspot.com.

Stolze, Dolly. "The Case of the Sausage Vat Murder and the Dissolved Wife." Strange Remains, 2014. https://strangeremains.com

Tennenbaum, Sara. "Laurie Dann: Timeline of 1988 Fires, Winnetka School Shooting, Standoff." ABC 7 Eyewitness News, May 17, 2018. https://abc7chicago.com

"The Murder of Jack McGurn." The St. Valentine's day Massacre, undated (no author) www.stvalentinemassacre.com

"The Grimes Sisters." The Theorem Factory, 2017 https://theoremfact.wordpress.com.

Thrilllist, "Chicagoland's Most Iconic Movie Homes." 2016 (no author). www.thrilllist.com

Truesdale, Jeff. November. 26, 2019. *The Last Words of Infamous American Killers: 'It's a Good Day to Die.'* People Magazine. https://people.com.

Uhlein, Mikhail. "The Marxes in Chicago." Marxology, (undated). www.marx-brothers.org

Ward, Joe. 2016. "Maybe OJ Simpson's Knife Wasn't in Chicago after All." DNA Info. www.dnainfo.com

Richard Speck. Undated. No Author. Wikipedia. https:/en.wikipedia.org

Silas Jayne. Undated. No Author. Wikipedia.org. https://en.wikipedia.org

Sam DeStefano. Undated. No Author. Wikipedia. https://en.wikipedia.org

Wischnowshy, Dave. 2020. *Celebrating Chicago's Starring Role in Filmmaking History.* Wisch List. http://wischlist.com.

Hilton Northbrook. Undated. No Author. WTTW Interactive. https://interactive.wttw.com.

Zabiegalski, Robin. 2017. *15 Things to Know about the Unsolved Murder of the Grimes Sisters.* The Talko. www.thetalko.com.

Endnote References

1. Unknown *Chicago Tribune* reporter. 1874.

2. Henderson, Harold. September 21, l989. Grave Mistake. *Chicago Reader.*

3.   Zumbach, Lauren. May 23, 2019. The Legacy of Flight 191. *Chicago Tribune.*

4.   Dwyer, Bill. August 14, 2007. Details of Spilatro murder revealed in trial. Oakpark.com.

5.   Holloway, Diane. 2001. Dallas and the Jack Ruby Trial, Memoir of Judge Joe B. Brown. Lincoln, NE: Author's Choice Press.

6.   Burrough, Brain. 2004. Public Enemies. New York: *The Penguin Press.*

7.   Dudek, Mitch. December 14, 2008. Where John Wayne Gacy buried the Bodies, more key sites tied to serial killer. *Chicago Sun Times.*

8.   Goad, Jim. 8 Dead Nurses in One Night: The Horrible Story of Richard Speck. *Thought Catalog.*

9.   William Heirens. *Wikipedia.org.*

10.   Zabliesko, Robin. 2017. 15 Things to know about the unsolved murder of the Grimes sister. *The Talko.*

11.   Keilman, John. January 8, 2013. Brown's Chicken Killings, 20 years ago today. *Chicago Tribune.*

12.   Pfeifer, Kelsey Grace. 2017. Ten things You Need to Know About the Original Playboy Mansion. Culture Trip.

13.   Allen, Steve. 1996. But Seriously: Steve Allen speaks his Mind. Amherst: *Prometheus Books.*

14.   Shales, Tom. October 14, 1996. Kim Novak: No Fear of Falling. *The Washington Post.*

15.   Burns, Ken. January 17, 2005. Unforgivable Blackness, Ghost in the House. *PBS.*

16.   Heston, Charlton. 1978. The Actor's Life. New York: *E.P. Dutton.*

17.   Medved, Harry and Michael. 1984. The Hollywood Hall of Shame: The Most Expensive Flops in Movie History. New York: *Perigree Books.*

18.   Caddie Hall of Fame. Murray Brothers. *WGA website.*

19.   Joe. l938-41. A Kid Named Bud: Marlon Brando in Libertyville. *Shelfie Life*, *Cook Memorial Public Library District Blog.*

20.   "Todd Seminary for Boys." *Wikipedia.*

21.   Dudek, Wayne. October 25, 2008. Orson Welles' Complicated Feelings about Kenosha. *Milwaukee Journal Sentinel.*

CPSIA information can be obtained
at www.ICGtesting.com
Printed in the USA
LVHW081927160920
666193LV00003B/35